THE CHOICE EFFECT

THE
CHOICE
EFFECT

Love and Commitment in an Age of Too Many Options

AMALIA MCGIBBON   LARA VOGEL   CLAIRE A. WILLIAMS

SEAL PRESS

The Choice Effect
Love and Commitment in an Age of Too Many Options

Copyright © 2010 by Amalia McGibbon, Lara Vogel, and Claire A. Williams

Published by
Seal Press
A Member of the Perseus Books Group
1700 Fourth Street
Berkeley, California

Library of Congress Cataloging-in-Publication Data

McGibbon, Amalia, 1982-
  The choice effect : love and commitment in an age of too many options / by Amalia McGibbon, Lara Vogel, and Claire A. Williams.
    p. cm.
  Includes bibliographical references.
  ISBN-13: 978-1-58005-293-1
  ISBN-10: 1-58005-293-2
  1. Man-woman relationships--Psychological aspects. 2. Women--Psychology.
  3. Choice (Psychology) 4. Commitment (Psychology) I. Vogel, Lara, 1982-
  II. Williams, Claire A., 1982- III. Title.
  HQ801.M336 2009
  306.7084'22090511--dc22
                                    2009039535

Cover design by Domini Dragoone and Kate Basart
Interior design by Megan Jones Design
Printed in the United States of America
Distributed by Publishers Group West

CONTENTS

INTRODUCTION:
A Theory Is Born

When we were freshmen in college, going on a date meant ditching the dining hall and getting the upperclassman with the '93 Corolla to drop us off at the Olive Garden. After slipping cheap vanilla vodka into our Shirley Temples and nodding along to stories of his renegade a cappella group, Just Duet, we waited on the curb for a ride back to our dorms. We could taste adulthood in the air.

Four years later, we'd amassed a few other significant experiences: getting and killing our first pet fish, taking an Italian lover while "studying" abroad, and laughing at people who bought class rings. We were on a roll, and soon we had real paychecks and real health insurance and real crappy apartments. We were in good relationships with good people. The rest of our lives—marriage, baby, house—seemed to be coming into focus. Ah, life, we would sigh with our friends, swishing Two Buck Chuck in mismatched coffee mugs. How urbane, how real, how sure we were.

"We have it figured out!" Everyone seemed to be shouting from rooftops.

Until they weren't.

Specifically, it started with one small individual breaking up with another small individual. At the time this seemed reasonable. Sad for Buffy and Biffy but *oh well*. Isolated incident. We all smiled. More shouting, different rooftops.

And then it started happening in droves.

George the consultant had broken up with Denise to pursue a screenwriting career. Or as Denise calls it, the job-that-will-never-amount-to-anything-but-I-hope-he-enjoys-his-mom's-basement.

Dina and Lisa had been doing long distance for the past year when Dina suddenly pulled the plug on their Skype connection, claiming it was "just the wrong time."

Sally said she loved Harry, but she wanted space. Lots of it. Like the kind they have in Nepal.

Joseph and Trini had been talking about engagement, but Joseph said since they were both Long Island Jews the relationship was too one-note. Suddenly they weren't talking at all.

The names may be fake, but the situations were real. Pretty soon, every time we turned our head some perfectly respectable couple was ending things. These were loving, functional, worth-your-resentment relationships that had suddenly hit a wall. "What the what?" we would say, at least once Tina Fey told us to.

We started surveying the landscape to detect where the relationship landmines were hidden. Everything seemed okay; people were well groomed and holding down jobs. But say the words "ten-year plan" or "ovaries" and most of our friends would just laugh nervously and start surfing Craigslist. Our own lives weren't any more according-to-plan, we have to admit. We were right alongside our peers, keeping up with seasonal career changes, around-the-world travel escapism, and an ever-growing catalog of exciting! (a.k.a. wrong-for-you) partners. Yep, with college degrees in hand, we had apparently hit the ground running . . . away from things.

Confused? Yeah, we were too. But that was before we spent twelve months banging our heads against our MacBooks trying to write this here *literature*. In a desperate attempt to validate our own behavior since college, we looked around and discovered an entire subset of the population—educated folks in their twenties and thirties—who were gluttons for options. We seemed unanimously set on avoiding any and all decisions.

In *The Choice Effect*, we'll explore the full measure of this phenomenon: how we acquired this optionful mind-set (parents! Mr. Rogers!), how we indulge it when single, and how we try to ignore it when dating. Central to this book is an exploration of all the sparkling choices out there competing for our attention—friends, dating, work, the range of MAC eye shadows, travel—and how these are at the heart of our generation's attitudes toward love and commitment.

In this book, we refer to "our generation" knowing full well that some of you may resist being defined, while others will be psyched to be back in a clique. Whether you're eighteen and beginning to sense that you might wallow in the muck of your murky future for a while or thirty-four and sick of people questioning your nontraditional life trajectory, this book is for you. We'll tell you about why we think you're a "choister" and why loving choice when the world is your oyster is really the only thing to do.

Of course we'll talk about the Ultimate Commitment—you know, the one that comes with a diamond and kitchen appliances. We'll discuss how, when it comes to marriage, our generation is stalling for longer and longer before making that leap, and what happens when we finally do get married, or when we choose not to. *The Choice Effect* celebrates our good fortune at having so many options and the potential to engineer exactly the life we want. But we warn you, this is nonfiction, so we also cast a glimpse at what we might be conceding along the way.

This book has not come without its ironic bitch slaps. Remember, yours truly are suffering the same "don't make us choose" disease, and it turns out writing a book requires a lot of decisions. Choosing a title was a struggle—one that echoed the romantic process we were describing. For every good title we came up with, we were convinced there'd be a better option around the corner. We only pulled the trigger after an all-night brainstorming session that left us back where we had been weeks before. But, as we told our parents, who watched our stalling in horror, we "valued the process" and "felt affirmed" (by what? by who? didn't matter) so it was all totally worth it. The same logic applies not only to book titles, it goes for every expectation we have for ourselves; the destinies we imagine we're supposed to fulfill are not limited to our choice of partner.

If *The Choice Effect* is "comic sociology" (we thank *New York Times* columnist David Brooks for this term, among others), then enter your favorite social comics: We are Amalia, Lara, and Claire. We met freshman year of college, and the past decade has seen us starring in our fair share of self-inflicted drama.

The idea for this book came to us at four in the morning in a tiny South African beach town when we were all at various stages of romantic distress—Claire and Lara with recent breakups, Amalia debating a cross-continental move. We were surrounded by dozens of books on love and dating that one member of our trio had dragged a bit too far across the Atlantic and another member of our trio was diligently berating as antifeminist trash. And there, with the help of a few requisite empty wine bottles, the choister theory was born. Although it wasn't called that at the time. The word, the idea, the book—have all evolved along with our own understanding of the unique predicament that ambitious, idealistic, and yes, self-aggrandizing young women find themselves in.

In some ways, the three of us are very similar. We like travel, we like not working in cubicles, we like men. We think *moist* is a bad word, we hate abnormally shaped fruit, and we cried tears of joy when Obama was elected. At the time of submitting this manuscript, we are all in serious relationships. At one point in the inherently long publishing process, one of us joked, "Shit, we can't all be married when this book comes out because that will really deflate our argument, and then Oprah won't invite us on her show." Another one of us countered that we better not all be broken up because Oprah sure as hell wasn't going to invite us anyway and breakups suck.

Clearly, we have different perspectives, and for good reason. Claire was born and raised in Berkeley, started nonprofit organizations in Africa before grabbing an MBA. She now works at Twitter and runs marathons like they're going out of style. Lara's vaguely hippie/puritan parents made her the lacto-vegetarian she is, but are lately intent on the message that marriage and kids are wonderful things (when they come together). After years of international wandering, Lara is homing in on becoming a doctor. Amalia's Jewish, her parents are divorced (but very friendly with one another!), and she writes about food for several San Francisco magazines. From London. And all these differences led us to dislike each other on the first day of freshman year, and to eventually become inseparable (well, at least by email) a decade later.

We've all been brokenhearted, but we cope with it differently—some with sex, some with religion, some with work, and all with travel and sobbing. We cover enough of the personality spectrum that you can trust at least one of us. (We're sure there's a probability theory that backs this up.)

But despite our army of three, we had to call in backup plenty of times because it turns out writing a book is hard. We exploited all those near and dear for help, with friends polled for every minor decision, grandparents proofreading for grammar, foreign boyfriends rooting for our efforts ("It's great! There is no boreness!"), and a lone American boyfriend pointing out that the show was never, ever called Sex *IN* the City. We held focus groups and baited people's anecdotes with wine and cheese. We surveyed over one hundred of our peers (aged nineteen to thirty-five, San Francisco to Italy, consultant to social worker) with questions like "How many sexual partners do you THINK you'll have before you marry?" and "Are you anxious about having children by a certain age?" We questioned Facebook friends to make sure the story we were telling wasn't only our own. We even approached Tyra Banks, Tina Fey, and Diablo Cody for comment—and although none of them felt compelled to write back per se, we feel their spirits are guiding our pen.

The Choice Effect is not a dating manual, a pop psychology self-discovery tour guide, a confessional tell-all, or an exposé on sex for the single girl. But it is intended to show you how this twentysomething century has made a twentysomething woman no one has seen before, provide a good laugh, and make our mothers proud. Because if we're not giving them grandkids any time soon, we better distract them with something....

CHOISTER? WHY DO YOU KEEP MAKING THAT FUNNY SOUND?

I was in the grocery store buying face wash, and it literally took me twenty minutes to decide between Neutrogena, Bioré, Dove, St. Ives, Clearasil, and Olay. If we translate this analogy to career decisions, marriage decisions, sexuality decisions, it may take us a lifetime to finally decide who we are and what we are doing.

—RUBY DARLING, AGE 23

Halloween has always been important to Claire, and in fourth grade this meant that the planning of her costume started in August. By the Big Night, it was down to a Welsh princess, a Teenage Mutant Ninja Turtle, and Tonya Harding. She had tried them all on, forced numerous fashion shows on her poor younger brother (already ensconced in his homeless person garb), and still couldn't decide. Claire's wee mind was scheming: Which one would get her the most candy? Which one would get Tommy from next door to think she was cute? It was a very difficult, protracted process. She didn't end up deciding until nine o'clock Halloween night, just in time to go out and get four pieces of candy before neighbors' stocks ran out.

Claire's parents looked on in confusion and gave away all their Halloween candy to the less obsessive children ringing their doorbell. Is she crazy? Is she "special"? Maybe a little bit of both, but we know two social psychologists who make us believe Claire's problems were within normal range.

In 2000, Drs. Sheena S. Iyengar and Mark R. Lepper set up a tasting booth at an upscale grocery in California. On some days, the researchers put out a selection of six types of jam; on other days they set out twenty-four. Lepper and Iyengar found that although the wider selection attracted more shoppers, more people bought the jam when there were fewer options. It seemed the more choices people had, the harder it was to make a decision.[1]

Now, this is not a book about Halloween or jam (two people just put the book down). Instead, this is a book that explores what happens when a sense of possibility invades every element of your life. It is a book about what is happening to the generation of people who have been stopped in their tracks by one of the biggest explosions of life options in recent memory.

Think about it. In the last few decades, our world has simultaneously expanded and become small enough to fit on a nanochip. Our perception of what's going on out there has deepened exponentially through the power of the Internet, which is currently curled up in your pocket waiting to be unleashed by a few taps on a touchscreen. And that's just the beginning. In today's world of brand-new globalization, technology, reproductive science, and redefined gender roles, we've entered the age of last-minute tickets to Moscow, test-tube children, cross-continental cubicles, and encouraged paternity leaves.

And what has come of this big bang boom of options? Us—a generation that loves choice and hates choosing. We've been called Generation Y, Millennials, Echo Boomers, the Internet Generation, and Nexters. A few of you probably identify with Gen X, too. We're somewhere between the ages of twenty and thirty-five. We were born at least a decade before anyone had email addresses, but are young enough to know what virtual cakes are on Facebook. Our childhoods chased the glory of *Reading Rainbow*, Cabbage Patch Kids, Duran Duran, bike shorts under skirts, jelly shoes (the first and second time), chokers, *Charles in Charge, Step by Step*, Baby-sitter's Club, R. L. Stine, and the lyrics to Salt-N-Pepa's "Shoop."

Today, Gen Y-ers fall somewhere between college and commitment. We buy our own diamonds and plan babies around our workloads. We pride ourselves on our full passports, close girlfriends, and "nontraditional" career paths. Essentially, we're the group of people who graduated into adulthood just in time to look around, see all those new, sparkly options at every turn, and realize we got to be the lucky ones to rip off the wrapping and give them a spin.

We can get a bit dizzy, what with all the unwrapping and spinning. In fact, there's such a thing as being over-choiced. We seem to love all these career, lifestyle, and personal options so much that we can't bear putting any one of them down. We know that there is nothing worse than leaving something behind only to realize later that it is exactly what we want. We're like little Lara when she played "Who should live?" as a child, a morbid game in which she would pretend the house was burning down and would try to snatch whatever belongings she deemed worth saving. True to the adult she would become, Lara always took too much and ended up tripping down the stairs.

Meg R., a twenty-nine-year-old medical school student, sums up what happens twenty years later: "I literally *can't* choose. I know that I need to do 'this,' and I need to do 'that,' and wish I was okay settling, but nothing is enough to make me do it . . . I'm physically incapable of compromising my expectations."

It's a given that every new generation will have more opportunities than the last. But once in a while, things really fast-forward. And for the choisters, even the term fast-forward is dated.

WHAT THE SHUCK'S A CHOISTER?

To give you a clear picture of what a choister is, we considered drawing something. But then we realized that we can't draw, and a poorly conceived oyster-man comic would only complicate something very simple:

choice + oyster = choister

Or, more formally: A choister is a person who is inundated with choices and thinks the world is his or her oyster. We, as a generation, got that last part from our parents and public service ads, which taught us to believe we could be anything we put our minds to. We, as authors, got that last part from Shakespeare, who introduced the winning "world is my oyster" phrase in *The Merry Wives of Windsor* in 1600. And if that's not enough of an academic diversion, the word "choice" is derived from the Old French word "chois," making our "choister" with an "s" inadvertently brilliant.

You could overanalyze Shakespeare's intended meaning, or the exact logic of that metaphor (do I have to shuck it myself?), but generally speaking, it's come to represent the belief that the world is yours for the taking.

Before this goes any further, we know you must be wondering— as we babble on about limitless options—how we are managing to ignore the daily facts of life like bills or rent. Is a trust fund a choister requirement? Not at all—and most of us only have two pennies to our name. But while we may face rough patches of unemployed, broke, lonely, or back on Mom's couch, we still have the perspective to see that these setbacks are nothing in the face of our embarrassment of fortune. Choisters are some of the most fortunate people on earth: They are those who have been lucky and safe enough to grow into educated and employable citizens of one of those comparatively rich nations where even crappy daily life at least comes with running water. So even if you're too busy heading to your two jobs to have ever consciously thought, "Which one of my beautiful options should I reach out and frisk today?" you are not excluded from the choister club.

So, no—our pocketbooks are not protected from the world's currently bursting economic bubble, but our mind-sets are. A year of financial panic or a bad term of unemployment can't beat twenty-seven years of feeling like the world is yours to go out and get. According to a recent USA Today/MTV poll, two-thirds of the eighteen- to twenty-nine-year-olds surveyed said they were "very or somewhat optimistic about the country's future."[2] See, we're not rich, we're just indoctrinated. No matter how pitiful Amalia's bank account becomes, she still evaluates professional options according to their "happiness quotient."

But even more to the point of this book is that our bank accounts and employment options have very little to do with whom we choose to marry and how we choose to love. So before you scoff at our insistence that we still have "too many options," remember that a recession will not affect the number of doable people in America. They say beggars can't be choosers. Luckily, we're neither.

Happy endings are not a given, and they are not something we're entitled to. But with more independence and more options than ever before, we truly believe that with just a bit of hard work, good behavior, and most importantly, the right choices, we will end up at some unprecedented level of happily ever after.

Choisters are hypnotized by options and can't imagine turning any of them down. The exact problem with choosing? It takes most of your choices off the table. And who knows what pearl you just gave away! So choisters work hard to avoid this eventuality, prioritizing the opportunity to choose before the choice itself.

Come—join us. It's cozy in here.

QUIZ: ARE YOU A CHOISTER?

I. After graduating from college, you

   a. moved back home and took unpaid internships to explore different careers;

   b. worked for Obama and/or became a community organizer;

   c. worked at a "groundbreaking" social networking start-up to fund your trip around the world;

   d. moved to a developing country to teach English and build houses.

2. When your first friend got married, you

   a. broke out in hives;

   b. wondered if she'd actually ever been inside a Williams-Sonoma before putting the entire store on her registry;

   c. drank a bottle of wine and Facebooked your middle school crush;

   d. found a new job and made it your bitch.

3. It is a valuable use of money to

   a. buy ten mojitos every week for five years;

   b. buy twenty goats for a shepherd in Guatemala;

   c. buy the Super Saver 500 Latte card so the coffee shop will let you use them as an office;

   d. rent an apartment for ten years.

4. You have a celebrity crush on

    a. Johnny Depp (or rather, Gilbert Grape);

    b. Steve Martin;

    c. Jon Stewart;

    d. John Krasinski.

5. You think that pharmaceutical sales is

    a. something related to the movie *The Constant Gardener*;

    b. a euphemism for crack dealer?

    c. the job that every female contestant on *The Bachelor* has;

    d. what the Man did to ruin Africa.

6. For your bat mitzvah, you got

    a. your first stock;

    b. a lesson about how wanting money is bad, but debt is worse;

    c. gifts from your eight grandparents;

    d. bitter. It sucks to be the only Episcopalian in New Jersey.

7. You look down on

    a. people who don't believe in global warming;

    b. people who don't know where Sudan is;

    c. people who have American flags on their lawn but think the Dixie Chicks should shut up;

    d. investment bankers.

8. **On Saturday mornings, you can be found**

   a. working (the promotion won't earn itself);

   b. out at brunch with three friends and ten side dishes;

   c. snuggled up in bed to the man you've been dating a week;

   d. snuggled up in bed to the man you've been dating six years.

9. **Your favorite movie is**

   a. *Juno;*

   b. *Garden State;*

   c. *Man on Wire* (okay, it's not your favorite movie yet, but you'll see it soon—100 percent on Rotten Tomatoes, baby);

   d. Will.i.am's "Yes We Can." (Wait—is that not considered a movie? But we watched it for more than two hours.)

10. **Your favorite book is**

    a. *Are You There God? It's Me, Margaret;*

    b. *The End of Poverty;*

    c. *Eat, Pray, Love;*

    d. *Freakonomics.*

Answers: All answers mean you are a choister. We told you choisters don't believe in choosing.

TALKING SMACK

Not everyone loves choisters as much as we love ourselves. Do you remember when you were five and that pigtailed biotch in the playground talked shit about your sparkly My Little Pony Velcro shoes? Your mother probably set the record straight: "Don't worry, honey, she's just jealous." With that one little phrase, your insecurities were banished and your confidence restored—you almost started pitying the girl for not having your natural fashion know-how. It's time to repeat that exercise twenty years later, without the Velcro.

We choisters know jealousy when we see it. Admit it, we've got a pretty sweet deal going on here—even when it does occasionally occur in Mom and Dad's basement. We're the most traveled, most career-versed, and most educated generation to come down the pike in a hybrid SUV. When Toys "R" Us launched its new "I don't want to grow up" jingle in the 1980s, it did more than just assault the ears of parents and elementary school teachers—it molded us. But fifteen years later, we've defied the jingle by simultaneously growing up *and* remaining Toys "R" Us kids. Sure, we've got checking accounts and college degrees, but there still are a million toys that we play with. We think that's impressive multitasking; naysayers scream that it's juvenile.

The primary criticism against us appears to be what a recent (bad) blockbuster referred to as our *Failure to Launch,* or rather, our extended holding pattern. Gen Y—or as we authors like to call ourselves Generation whY Not Later—has become infamous for its inability to get on with things and to graduate to real live spouse-picking, child-birthing adulthood. From prime-time television shows about moving back home (we deeply resent the title of Fox's *Free Ride*—living with your parents is *never* free) to *Time* articles labeling us betwixters and betweeners, we are constantly being told that we have run amok.

A *Wall Street Journal* article by Jeffrey Zaslow called us "the most praised generation," and another article in *The Advertiser*, entitled "Y Kids Just Know They're Fabulous," offered these precious tidbits: "They are famously known as the generation who expect everything, and give zero."[3, 4] Meanwhile, a recent CBS News story interviewed various Baby Boomers for their opinions on us younger folk. Marian Salzman, one of the top five trendspotters in the world, claims, "You do have to speak to them a little bit like a therapist on television might speak to a patient." She adds, "You can't really ask them to live and breathe the company. Because they're living and breathing themselves and that keeps them very busy."[5, 6]

Dr. Jean Twenge, author of *Generation Me: Why Today's Young Americans Are More Confident, Assertive, Entitled—And More Miserable Than Ever Before*, posits that the average college student is 30 percent more narcissistic in 2006 than she or he would have been in 1982.[7]

These are not very nice things to say. And according to some, our hubris doesn't translate well in the realm of romance. To put it more bluntly, "That kind of grandiosity eats relationships," says therapist Terry Real, in an interview with The Daily Beast.[8] The article's author, Hannah Seligson, continues, "Twentysomethings not only expect to waltz into high-level career positions right out of college, they also expect partners who have . . . the comedic timing of Stephen Colbert, the abs of Hugh Jackman, and the hair of Patrick Dempsey."[9] Now, that's just *NOT* true. Any one of those fellows, with all their own parts, can come visit us at our high-powered offices any day.

Jen Schefft, a contestant who vied for Andrew Firestone's love on the only season of *The Bachelor* that anyone cared about, has been a favorite punching bag for the media. When Schefft reappeared as The Bachelorette post-Firestone, she chose none of the twenty-five male suitors, even turning down two marriage proposals. When a celebrity magazine remarked that she would be "a bachelorette for the rest of her life,"[10] it showed that the high standards of choisters threaten certain societal structures that others find important . . . to their masculinity (just a guess).

Even some of our peers are putting a negative slant on things. The book *Quarterlife Crisis,* by Abby Wilner and Alexandra Robbins, argues that the twenties and thirties are "essentially a period of anxiety, uncertainty, and inner turmoil that often accompanies the transition to adulthood."[11]

But is that the life we're leading? It doesn't *feel* that bad. Now, we won't lie—there's stress and indecision, and "quarterlife crisis" definitely speaks to certain dark moments in dark corners with dark liquors. But that's not the whole of it. For the most part, we believe twenty- and thirtysomethings revel in their choices and feel lucky to have them. And because of that, we won't settle for settling down. *Quarterlife Crisis* also argues that troubles in this time of life come from not knowing yourself; author Alexandra Robbins says: "We don't really know what we want, so we don't know how to get it."[12] But *we* argue that we *do* know what we want . . . we want everything, and it just takes some time to fit it all into our tiny apartments. Perhaps you think we're calling one problem by another name, but the difference between the two is significant, and it has a lot to do with who's moping in that corner and who's out in the world.

Choisters know we're a blessed generation and sometimes feel self-conscious of our luck. There's a lot of "Oh, it's nothing" when we mention our latest job, boyfriend, or opportunity because our richness of choices can be a bit ridiculous. Turns out some of our faux modesty has come back to bite us, as our parents occasionally do think we're just fucking around. While enjoying your little life shopping spree, you have likely heard one of the following criticisms from your parents since graduating from college:

- Stop creating bizarre small businesses out of jewelry making, viral video directing, and lacrosse coaching. Definitely stop making more than one.

- Stop opening so many windows/tabs on your computer at once—learn to focus.

- Stop thinking a blog is a job.

- Stop spending your weekends with girlfriends unless they have husbands and can inspire you to want them too.

- Stop dumping guys because they don't give you the same butterflies in your stomach that Obama did.

If we were taking our lives seriously, they say, we would have children on the way or within sight, and a career focused on just ONE professional passion that started at the ripe age of twenty-two. If it's not marriage to a person, then at least marry *something:* choose choose choose, the world is yelling.

No no no.

WHY WE WON'T MARRY NOTHIN' YET

It's hard to put down the pretty toys. Or the pretty boys. It's not that we can't eventually pick a favorite—it will just take something very shiny and special to pull us away from the combined glare of everything else.

For Gen Y-ers, it became clear at about age eight—when we were first introduced to the girl who has gadgets and gizmos aplenty, whozits and whatzits galore—that even mermaids can get swanky lives on land. If a young woman with a fish tail won't settle for anything less than a species switch, then why should we? No, we want the happily-ever-after ending, replete with proud father and jealous sisters.

The only snag, the only reason why it's not full steam ahead toward the final credits, is that there are too many Erics. Too many rocks to perch our lithe bodies upon. When you have all the opportunities in the world, it's rather hard to pick just one.

Bari S., a twenty-one-year-old photographer in Colorado, empathizes: "It's not that I am unmotivated or led by chance, quite the opposite. I have so many goals and aspirations that I cannot imagine spending the rest of my life in one career, with one person, in one country. Marriage seems like a game of poker to me; the only way you can really win is if you know the hand of every other player involved. Why waste my royal flush on someone who turns out to be a three of a kind?"

Which explains why so many fantastic relationships are ending. The looming possibility of marriage, of *choosing* a single person (or two or three for you polyamorists out there), is enough to make you head back to sea.

Sorry, team, but the value of "together forever" is dropping with no bailout in sight. A recent study found that 57 percent of eighteen- to twenty-four-year-olds surveyed agree with the statement, "The institution of marriage is dying in this country."[13] Well, no wonder, considering how many of us (tens of millions, in fact) spend our days reading up on single celebrity moms and famous divorces on PerezHilton or Dlisted. The idea of "happily ever after" has taken a few shots of realism, and we've come to accept the idea that it is our readiness, more than some crazy soul spark with a guy, that will determine our agreement to, or at least the timing of, a wedding.

Interestingly, it appears that the women of our generation are leading this redefinition of marriage. Women are "less likely [than men] to believe parents must be married," says a recent Greenberg poll, as well as "much more likely [than men] to question marriage as a way of life . . . and more discouraged about prospects in their peer group."[14] Marriage and commitment do have value. Heck, in some respects the stakes are at an all-time high, and we care enormously about giving Ellen and Portia the opportunity to tie every knot their hetero counterparts do. However, one thing is clear: Marriage and commitment are no longer a measure of maturity, or a necessary checkpoint on the road to happiness or adulthood.

Look at the numbers. In 1959, 47 percent of all brides were under nineteen.[15] And according to *The New York Times*, the median age for first marriages has risen dramatically in the last thirty-five years, "from 23 for men and 21 for women in 1970 to 27.5 for men and 25.5 for women in 2006."[16] When we polled our peers, more than 85 percent said that they believed they would get married older than when their parents did. Not only are people getting married later, they're doing it less often. Between 1970 and 1996, the rate of marriage in the US fell from seventy-seven marriages per one thousand unmarried women to fifty marriages per one thousand unmarried women—a drop of one-third.[17]

The times, they are a-changin'—again. It was recently reported that only 7 percent of eighteen- to twenty-five-year-olds are "very worried" about finding a spouse, compared to 35 percent who are "very worried" about getting an STD and 33 percent who are "very worried" about landing a job when they graduate from college.[18] Choisters tend to find themselves in situations where Grandma pulls them aside for a talk about their "special someone" and they think she's asking about their boss. And while you're probably better educated than your parents, they manage to trump those turns in the conversation by pointing out that at your age, they had already birthed you.

People are marrying later or not at all, people are breeding later or not at all, and people are dating around in ways even our free-loving parents can't get their collective mind around. We seem to be baffling everyone. We have an unprecedented chance to make everything easy—women are (more) equal; minority opportunities are (hopefully maybe) on the rise; everyone's making more money (until recently); the unofficial caste system with its severe English undertones has broken down. Our moment has come! Time to live the dream! And then we throw everyone off by popping the Pill and hoping Johnny doesn't propose.

Our mothers laugh and say all our prioritizing of travel, work, and lifestyle will go out the window once the biological clock starts ticking. We say we know a great fertility specialist who can take care of that. Our fathers point out that we still would prefer a husband with money and drive than one without. We say who needs a husband? I have a job I love (or at least a promising job concept in mind), a 401(k), and a sperm donor friend. It surely sounds a bit like devil's advocate, but these are nonetheless the conversations going on in the trendy wine bars we over-frequent.

YOU TALKING TO ME?

Anyone anywhere can be a choister. If you've got options and want to keep them open, you're in the club. But in this book we are speaking particularly to those whose minds are so abrim with choices—I heart boys . . . no, girls! Doctor . . . no, ad exec! Bali . . . no Barcelona!!—that they are perhaps a bit overwhelmed in the face of all they could be. To you, getting the best means never settling. And it certainly means not sacrificing one thing for another. Understandably, this mentality is starting to wear a bit on the lovers and the elders in your life who think committing to one thing is the Only Adult Thing to do. But they'll live.

Choisters can be men or women. But this book is about women. Sorry, boys, it's just that choisterness—at least as it pertains to relationships—is harder to detect in you because it seems to blend with your natural, socially validated "mojo." Men have always wanted to spread their seed, and society has always told them to enjoy doing so, making it difficult to distinguish choisterism from primal mating behavior. If Simba has sex with five different lionesses, he's not a choister—he's just a lion.

For some women, the choister way is a natural calling, while others had first loves they would have married if given the chance.

The latter group was too busy doodling hearts to think about "options." But then some commitment-phobic boyfriend decided he wanted to be an ex-boyfriend, and suddenly there we were. What began as a coping mechanism—"Oh fine, I'll go on this date just to get my mind off my one true love"—turned into a way of life—"What true love? I like me some dates!" It could be either curiosity or young heartache that threw you into the arms of your partners, but either way men have laid down some pretty thorough choister groundwork when it comes to a fear of commitment. Add to that the modern societal blessing to take on a bit more of those previously male behaviors, and *bam!* you've choisterized the last woman standing.

This book focuses on the topic that is slowly morphing MTV's *Real World* into softcore porn: the Herculean successes and disastrous results that come when a choister is set free in the world of dating and mating. And remember, it's not that we're unwilling to undergo the marriage/career/procreation rites of passage our parents experienced, we just don't want to inherit their timeline.

And we don't have to. In today's world, we choisters have a theme park's worth of options at our feet—why would we turn our back on all that variety for one thing if it's not The Very Best?

WHY WRITE A BOOK ABOUT IT? THAT'S, LIKE, A LOT OF WORK

So we've brought the Wii sword down on both your shoulders and bestowed a title upon you. But as a member of a fairly irreverent generation that eschews titles, you probably didn't want it in the first place. But we're hoping it will give us a handle with which to carry you through the full explanation of our behavior. That leaves your hands free to bring along snacks.

This new time of life ain't a bad thing, and don't let anyone tell you otherwise. In the wise words of Amalia, if this is a "crisis," then we didn't wear black pants and stretchy tank tops at college parties. (Read: This is definitely not a crisis.) A lot has been written about us, but it is now time to declare out loud, with catchphrases, that we are decidedly not juveniles, marriage haters, or ostriches with our heads in the sand of worldly distractions.

Because what if it really is smart to take time off after nineteen years of school? Or what if work productivity really does go up when you start getting rid of *Office Space*–esque bosses and cubicles alike? And, given the state of most of our parents' unions, maybe it really makes good sense to put off and/or reevaluate the whole marriage thing. Maybe we're just being smart and doing what we've been taught to: looking both ways before we cross.

The explosion of choices available to us has impacted our desires and expectations and led us to reconsider traditional decisions. We're simply reevaluating our options, and like every generation before ours, trying to make the best out of what we have. They say when you've got lemons, make lemonade. This book is about what happens when you just picked up lemons, sugar, flour, butter, vanilla extract, and a bottle of Boone's Farm.

MOMMY, WHERE DO CHOISTERS COME FROM?

2

My mother married my father because he promised her that she would never again have to work and that he would buy her a couch. Here I am on the opposite side of the spectrum, with a wonderful, understanding, intelligent boyfriend who would propose at the drop of a hat. However, I keep stalling because what if ten years down the line we are no longer compatible, I meet someone whom I should have married, et cetera.

—HARPER THOMAS, AGE 24

We get it. Parents say that "kids today" can't make decisions, the media accuses us of an extended adolescence, and the world at large seems to believe that we're simultaneously slacking off and reaching too high. Much like women in the nineteenth century who were misdiagnosed with "hysteria" and prescribed a pelvic massage, we see that if you're behaving in a way that society is unprepared for (say, choosing to work eighty-hour weeks over planning a wedding), you will be branded as odd, uppity, or chemically imbalanced.[1]

Happily, we were raised with enough Freudian sense to immediately blame everything on our parents and then use the term "psychological complex" to make ourselves sound smart. (Psychological complex! We said it!) Therefore, in the age of choister critiques, we evoke ten-year-old Amalia's clever defense when reprimanded by her parents for doing anything untoward: "But Mom, I am a product of my upbringing." Bratty? Yes. True? Entirely.

This isn't a book about our parents, but we've been in therapy too long *not* to ponder the role our mothers and fathers played in all this. Plus, they say "Know thine enemy," and in this case the enemy is delivering some very low blows to try to get grandkids. If we want to understand what's going on inside our heads, it's helpful to look at how we were raised and who did the raising. So now we travel back in time. Bear with us; this isn't a history lesson. Think of it more like a flashback in the middle of a *Friends* episode. Maybe we'll even toss in a fat suit.

INTRODUCING MOM AND DAD

So who are our parents? According to *New York Times* columnist and author David Brooks, who wrote a book about (roughly) our parents' generation, they're the "Bobos," or the bourgeois bohemians.[2]

They grew up in the 1950s and '60s, when the home was a temple, the mother a domestic goddess, and the husband a suited bread-winner. Our grandfathers had nine-to-five jobs and a penchant for rye whiskey, while Grams stayed at home—the beauty of no war or crop to tend to—and doted on our sweet, then-chubby-kneed parents. Think Leo and Kate's *Revolutionary Road*, with only half the depression and less clever arguing. It was in this now-stereotyped subsection of Americana that our parents came of age, and at the beginning they bowed their heads for every crew cut and tried to color inside the lines.

One would have expected them to take well to such a lifestyle. There was nothing inherently wrong, after all, with Mrs. Cleaver's Monday morning pancakes and a white picket fence. (We love pan-cakes and consider our own lack of Monday morning Bisquick no small burden to bear.)

But apparently it wasn't a good fit, and our parents proceeded to make a mess of the status quo. They don't call the '60s a time of *counterculture* for nothing. There was the sexual revolution, the drug revolution, and all that rock 'n' roll. Civil rights, women's rights, and the right to not wear a boulder holder followed in short suc-cession. Our parents—the same ones who wring their hands when we do things differently than they'd hoped—overthrew the rules of *their* parents by smoking weed for breakfast and having promiscu-ous hippie sex for lunch. An exaggeration? Not according to *Hair*.

All our grandparents wanted was for Billy to skip the protest and take Mrs. O'Malley's pretty daughter out on a date. Marriage and stability had been their holy grail, and they wanted that peace of mind for their children. Virginia H., who is in her midtwenties, had a mother who went straight to law school from college in the 1970s.

"I know my mom's parents were mad that she wasn't married in college," Virginia says, "and made it clear that her goal in law school should be an MRS degree." (That's going from *Miss* to *Mrs.*) Stacy S. R., twenty-five, tells a similar story: "My grandparents all grew up in the Depression, so of course they were of the mind-set that after you graduate from college you have to get on with your life and make sure you're stable." Or take Caroline B., twenty-seven, whose grandfather would lecture her about dating around too much. "When I was young," her grandfather would begin, "just finding a good, loving, trustworthy partner was enough." He would then downshift to remembering how he had walked uphill both ways to school.

But with more discontent and fewer STDs in the air, the time was ripe for a rebellion, and we honestly don't blame our parents for getting on the copious-amounts-of-sex-with-multiple-partners train (or at least watching and waving as it went by). By the time that train jumped the tracks and our parents were ready to settle down, they were getting married two to five years older than their parents had.[3] A big jump for one little generation to make.

As they turned toward middle age, these freewheeling Boomers invariably had to start acting like those upright folk they had worked so hard not to become. The same people who once defended their own right to wear suits made of flowers were suddenly yelling up the suburban stairs at us to "turn off all that noise!" as we angstily blasted Tom Petty's "You Don't Know How It Feels" on repeat.

But just because certain slices of life looked familiar, it didn't mean that times hadn't changed. Indeed, these middle-aged ex-hippies are now not only our parents but also the Establishment—though it is a far cry from the Establishment of yore. Say hello to today's educated, middle- to upper-class America: It's a world of NYTimes.com junkies who get buzzed on soy skim lattes and six-packs of California rolls before hot yoga. They balance stock reports and aromatherapy, take you wine tasting in Napa for your twenty-first, and fund your semester abroad in Beijing/Paris/Dubai.

We choisters are not claiming we invented exotic travel, endless education, and all things organic. Instead, we've apparently just taken it one or two degrees past where our parents took it thirty years ago. Which is why we're so confused: How can the people who urge us to find the homemade sandals they loved in Greece in 1970 get so frustrated when we're spending too much time traveling and not enough time decorating our cubicle? To reference David Brooks's term, it's the bohemian in them telling us to live it up and the bourgeois in them telling us to buckle down.

They've molded us in their own image, which means we're a contradiction too. And two contradictions do *not* an agreement make. So they encourage us to travel and then yell about our debt. They suggest we date around and then worry about all the sex we must be having. They tell us to leave jobs we hate and then throw up their hands at family reunions because Junior can't figure it out. "She's finding herself" is the catchphrase our parents use alternately as a compliment and a criticism.

In the words of a poorly translated T-shirt Claire purchased in Argentina: YOU'RE NOT THE ONLY ONE WITH MIX [sic] EMOTIONS.

AND THEN ALONG CAME US

Let's jump back to the moment when we entered the frame. After our parents were done having free-love sex (or, technically, in the midst of it—eeew), they made us. And we were the all-organic, pesticide-free, non-GMO apples of their eyes. While their own parents were known for polishing outward appearances (pumps as casual footwear), ours were equally obsessed with cultivating our interiors. They even warned us not to lose confidence if the Big Bad World judged our looks, and they cautioned us away from the fashion magazines our mothers routinely bought "for the recipes."

The luxury of such interior cultivation came partially from the fact that the quality of a child's future was no longer quite as predetermined by the beauty, status, fortune, and breeding of the parents, as it had been for so many generations.[4] Our parents were the first to fully realize that children can have bad self-esteem no matter how big their home is, that rich people do wear Birkenstocks, and that entrance into college—that critical step toward success—has been aggressively and publicly remodeled to be more about performance than pedigree. The redefinition of success was raining down! Dropouts could make millions! Actors could become president!

We're not saying that elitism is dead, or that obscene chunks of money don't buy you entrée into country-club clambakes, but our parents raised children in a world where social status was more fluid than ever before. Mom and Dad celebrated the opening of this back-door access to power and accomplishment and vowed to make the most of it for their young tots. Since my child is a genius/prodigy/unique snowflake, they reasoned, he or she can *make* his or her own success. If given the right opportunities to grow and flourish, there is no door that won't open for my kid! Enter Baby Mozart and private nursery schools. Our grooming began early, and mantras that we could be anything we wanted to be ricocheted off nursery walls.

President Obama—a billboard for the evolution of opportunity—gave this very sermon at the start of his presidency. Upon assuming the presidency, he wrote an open letter to his daughters in *Parade Magazine.* "These are the things I want for you—to grow up in a world with no limits on your dreams and no achievements beyond your reach," he wrote, echoing our own parents, who did everything they could to guarantee us the world. (Except write an open letter in *Parade Magazine.* Way to drop the ball, Dad.)[5]

THEY WHISPERED SWEET EVERYTHINGS

We can't claim that our parents loved us more than any other past generation loved its spawn, but they certainly *talked* about that love more. At every turn, there was a confidence-building remark—especially for the girls. "Good try, honey!" Claire's parents said when she couldn't do a somersault. Or, whenever Lara's parents wanted to lift her spirits, "The boys are just intimidated because you're so pretty." True or not (in Lara's case, not), the positive reinforcement rained down, and we lapped it up.

Amalia's stepfather always called her a "golden girl," a self-fulfilling reference to the fact that everything always seemed to go her way. And though this made her feel special, and she casually dropped it into conversation whenever possible, her friends weren't that impressed—their parents had similar nicknames for them. Cathy H., who has never met Amalia, would be similarly unimpressed: "Parents say we're really special and have a lot of gifts to offer; we're living in a meritocracy and are taught you can do anything you put your mind to."

Ours is a world of increased competition, and with two-year-olds going head-to-head for the last preschool spot and too much attention paid to spelling bee champions, it is even more critical that all kids know they're winners at home. Luckily, we did, because in a new twist, our parents made us feel not only loved, but *liked*. Allegedly, there is a biological mandate that you experience some sort of unconditional love for your offspring, but our parents harbored an affection that was clearly conditional...on our awesomeness! Because "liking" isn't a given. Just ask Claire's middle-aged childhood baby sitter, whose dislike for her own children prompted her to join a support group for people who don't like their kids (making her an obvious choice for a babysitter). For our parents, "liking" means thinking your kids are cute as babies, but being more excited for when they can talk and tell you what they're thinking. "Liking" means your kids are your friends and you can't think of a better way to spend a Saturday night than watching encores of their made-up dance routines. Okay, our parents never said those exact words, but you could see as much in their eyes.

What makes this far more impressive to us is that it's not like our parents had nothing better to do than sit and talk with an eight-year-old. Odds are that both your mom and dad worked. Hard. But they still tried to steal breakfasts and bedtimes with you whenever their adult responsibilities would tolerate the inconvenience. When Caitlin T. was five years old, her recently divorced mother invented "special time"—a one-hour playdate between mother and child, which began after Caitlin's three-year-old sister had gone to sleep. This helped Caitlin to be less bitter about the presence of her sibling, a.k.a. Attention Robber. But looking back on it now, Caitlin's most struck by the amount of willpower it must have taken for a thirty-five-year-old single mom to crack open *James and the Giant Peach* at nine o'clock instead of sending her daughter to bed and passing out herself. Nothing says love like Roald Dahl on a work night.

Obviously, blissful childhoods are not a choister prerequisite, and we are definitely only discussing one perspective on our childhood experience. Believe us, it wasn't always like living in a Sunny D commercial. But many of our parents held themselves to a ridiculously high standard: attending every PTA meeting, soccer game, and child therapy session. They were told to be heavily involved in our lives from the very beginning, and by our teens, Mom started trying to be "friends" with us—complete with inappropriate sexual trivia from her own past and attempts to join in chats about school dynamics. For all our blushing and "Mo-ooms!"—we knew we were lucky. Soon enough, kids started calling their parents (and other people's parents) by their first names, and the prioritization of the quality of the relationship between parents and children reached an all-time high.[6]

Choisters look at the über-functional family of *The Wonder Years* and marvel at the rapport: Hierarchies were so strict! Rules so inflexible! By comparison, the Huxtables' daughter had dreadlocks, Mitch Leery on *Dawson's Creek* was almost cool, and the Gilmore girls shared a closet. By the time *The OC* came around, we were old hands at watching daughters prep *mothers* for first dates. While Sarah Palin and her pit bull might argue that this progression reflects the deterioration of the American family, we posit that it actually just shows that the parent-child relationship is reaching beyond the dinner table into the daily lives of the family members.

It didn't help our ego control that when we looked to the outside world to check the validity of all this parental fawning, we found only more affirmation. Remember *Mr. Rogers' Neighborhood* and all those daily declarations that we were "special" for just being whoever we were? Although the show ran from 1968 to 2001, it hit its peak in 1985, when American households tuned in daily to watch Mr. Rogers and his fine friend Mr. McFeely (who the hell thought *that* was a good character for youngsters?) talk about how amazing we choister babes really were.[7] Of course we tuned in—and our parents encouraged it. When Mom and Dad were too tired to live up to the hype, they liked having some support staff at the ready.

People go so far as to argue that choisters were special even before they were born. Because for the first time, we're mostly a generation of planned children. As Jean M. Twenge points out in her book *Generation Me*, reliable birth control helped make ours "the most wanted generation of children in American history."[8] Neil Howe and William Strauss, authors of *Millennials Rising*, even coined the term "Kinderpolitics" to represent the political will in 1980s America that pushed for aggressive public policy on everything that would affect the nation's children, including things like crime and education.[9] Hell, we're so special we didn't even need lobbyists to catch Washington's eye.

Our parents did their best, trying out new tactics (speak more, spank less) to turn us into the brightest glow-in-the-dark star ever to go on a ceiling. We were told we could have it all, and we were taught to enjoy taking it. No worries: Grandma also taught us to say thank you.

EDUCATION: THE ULTIMATE EGO BOOST

Education proved a pretty direct means of delivering the self-esteem Kool-Aid. Montessori schooling and Waldorf education systems sprang up like optimistic new hairs on Natalie Portman's bald head, and *The Oregon Trail* slowed down early-stage Mac computers the world over.

The collective parental emphasis on achievement ushered in a new era of academic competition: Apply to private kindergarten? Obviously! Hire an SAT tutor and take the test ten times? Who doesn't? But the secret sauce on every school application? Extracurriculars! Show us a child of our generation, and we will show you someone with respectable experience in bocce ball, belly dancing, or Inuit. Choisters enjoyed the basic soccer/ballet/gymnastics package, but there was usually a piece of flair on the side: viola where violin was too common, klezmer band rather than school band. Who didn't want to play cricket at age seven?

Our parents pushed away thoughts of their most recent bank statements and remained dedicated to the long-term goal: college, a.k.a. the establishment of good life-launching pad and proof of child's educational maturity and independence. Many parents became a bit too involved in the application process. But heck, if you were saving for college for *two decades,* wouldn't you want your child to go to the best school possible? Wouldn't you also chain Randy to the desk until he *handwrote* his personal statement to Brown University? (If this example means nothing to you, celebrate the fact that you weren't trying to study in Rhode Island at the dawn of this millennium.)

Thankfully, more colleges were springing up to match this demand. In 1960, there were around 2,000 institutions of higher learning in the United States; by 1980 the number had jumped to 3,200.[10] And our enrollment matched this growth, as the number of women in institutions of higher education more than doubled from 1970 to 1995.[11] Nowadays, average tuition is up to a staggering $25,143 at private four-year universities and $6,585 at public four-year universities—both up by more than 5 percent from last year despite recessioning the world over.[12] Choisters can't help but be honored by this expensive vote of confidence. Your brain is worth a house, was the message. Your potential is worth adding another ten years to our retirement age. Nothing strokes your ego like knowing your parents are tens-of-thousands-of-dollars-they-*don't*-have sure of you.

HAPPINESS: THE NAIL IN THE COFFIN

But back to the 1980s and all our growing pains. The emphasis on über child achievement started early, causing reputable psychologists to raise a red flag. Many of us were in after-school programs five to six days a week and were as overenriched as the bread we ate. What about the old days, when children played with lizards in the grass and jumped off roofs for fun? In preparing us for a lifetime of achievement, our parents could be harming us?[13]

A general movement toward "child satisfaction" was born, in which children's happiness became paramount. This is where we get into teams of school counselors, girls' self-esteem classes, and the wonderful phenomenon of grade inflation. (Woot! Woot!) But even with the arrival of this movement, our parents weren't short-sighted enough to think trophies and grades didn't matter. Our parents faced an impossible tightrope act: "Aren't A's fun? Well, sure, so are B's, if that's what feels comfortable. Just do your best! Or how about a bit better?" School therapists suddenly became prophets to our parents, preaching how they could get Sally to just adore working hard.

With armies of people focused on making sure we were not only excelling but also loving every minute, we got their message loud and clear: You are not mediocre. Every step of your life should serve the purpose of providing meaningful joy and/or getting you somewhere amazing. We caught on quick: Happiness is what happens on your way toward achievement. Who wouldn't accept such a mission?

By the time we reached adolescence, our parents' message had been inscribed upon our consciousness, and we took it and ran out of the big white graduation tent and into our adulthood.

MOMMY, ARE CHOISTERS TOO HEAVY FOR THE STORK TO CARRY?

Which brings us to our love lives. And our parents. Together. In one paragraph.

Sometime before we ran away with our diplomas, every choister parent had to bite the bullet and tell us about that *other* kind of satisfaction. Everyone does the birds-and-bees conversation differently: Amalia and her mother had some overly close heart-to-hearts, while Claire's mother let her watch *Thirtysomething* and *Sisters*. Lara's embarrassed hyperventilation at her mother's first conversation attempt prompted the purchase of "Why Do I Feel Funny?" a Q-and-A style sex-ed manual Lara was to study at her own pace. All things considered, though, we had it comparatively easy, as we've heard tales of parents employing puppets.

However, no matter how or what you teach 'em, Baby Girl Choisters grow up eventually. And then they have sex. And their parents drop the puppets in horror.

In many ways, the iron curtain has been lifted from the dating world. Scandalous television (*Californication, Sex and the City, The*

L Word), presidential scandals, and Viagra spam have fully enlightened the public sexual consciousness. Great for us choisters—tough for Mom and Dad. Free love is groovy until it's your daughter who's giving it away.

When it comes to parents' reactions to their kids' dalliances, there seems to be a range of coping mechanisms. First, there's the "Ignorance Is Bliss" camp, represented by the parents of Elizabeth B., twenty-seven, a consultant in Boston. She explains, "When I told my mother about my first boyfriend at the age of eighteen, her response was a thirty-second lecture on the advantages of the Pill. Since then, they have been supportive—but mute—bystanders to my dating game." Shana W., twenty-seven, offers a similar perspective: "My parents always seemed very positive about the way I led my dating/relationship life, but to be honest, they never really offered an opinion one way or the other." Maria T.'s parents had found their *own* parents so insufferably opinionated during their courtship thirty years ago that they agreed on a strategy of silence: "They veered to the opposite extreme," Maria says, "and stayed away from encouraging or discouraging any particular behavior."

And then there's the other side of the field—the "Huddle up! What's Our Game Plan?" group, where everybody wants a say. Meg R.'s father is abnormally direct: "Meg, your twenties are for fucking all the wrong guys." Allison P.'s mom is always reminding her that it's good to meet new people. "And when I tell her that I've started to date someone," Allison says, "she'll make it sound overly casual, like, 'Well, you guys are just good friends, right?'" Lucy M.'s mom pulled out the big guns and volunteered to help her design a Match.com profile. "They're *strong* supporters of me getting out there and meeting people," says Lucy, as if it's an understatement.

And while choisters actually listen to advice from their parents—90 percent of our generation describes their relationship with their mother as close—it's difficult when the messaging is so mixed.[14] Amanda M., thirty-one, gives her perspective: "Both my parents say 'Who are we to tell you what to do?' but my mom does this thing—it's built into her speech—where marriage is this culmination that I no longer believe it is. But at the same time, she's also said things like, 'Don't forget that your twenties are an extended adolescence!'"

Twenty-nine-year-old Cynthia H.'s family has never pressured her outright about getting married, "but they've started to joke about me ending up a spinster or my younger sister getting married first." Hysterical. Angelica S., twenty-seven, has traditional parents who can't make up their minds: "My dad would be content if I were in a nunnery, and my mother would like for me to be married and with child." Elizabeth B., who was married this year at the age of twenty-seven, says, "My parents' concern with marriage generally centered on the idea of getting married too young. On the other hand, as soon as I was married they started arguing against waiting to have kids."

Our parents are all over the map. At least with our grandparents the rules were simple: (1) If you sleep with a guy you are loose forever, and (2) Be married by twenty-three, or you are a spinster. Easy to understand, if not to follow. You knew where you stood. But when our mothers say "How's the chemistry?!" and "He doesn't come all the way to the door?" in the same breath, it's more difficult to find your balance.

With such mixed messages, who can blame us for feeling confused about what template to follow? While we're generally very independent when it comes to dating, choisters can't help but be influenced by our parents' example and outlook. Of course, it's good to remember that our parents' love lives aren't always the toast of the town—especially once lawyers are part of the celebration.

THE D-WORD, OR, DO AS I SAY, NOT AS I DO

After Mommy put down the book of fairytales at night, there's a 50 percent chance she walked right into the other room to discuss a pending separation with Daddy. This means we had to read into two sets of lessons: what our parents intended to teach us and what they *accidentally* taught us.

Divorce, we argue, was one of those unintentional, this-isn't-what-I-meant lessons. With divorce rates fluctuating between 40 and 50 percent in the late '90s, choisters' childhoods were rife with "Mommy and Daddy have something to tell you" conversations.[15] Some of these divorces happened very early on, so bouncing between two homes was a way of life, while others occurred when we went to college, leaving us to question everything we'd ever known. The frequency of these separations certainly adds an addendum to our ideas about marriage. After all, it's hard to envision your own happily ever after when Mom and Dad's so clearly wasn't. Carrie G., twenty-nine, watched her mom suffer through two horrible divorces—one when Carrie was ten and the other just two years ago, and she says, "I don't go out into the world and think, *I don't want to get married.* I go out into the world and think, *I don't want to get divorced.* Because even with marriage, nothing is guaranteed. And now I'm watching my sixty-year-old mother at home alone every night, and she tried to find someone to grow old with, and it just didn't work."

Divorce isn't always toxic. Many separated parents are civil, even friendly, and some experts have argued it's healthier for kids to be party to no marriage than a bad one. And if at least one parent ends up truly happy in the remarried or revised situation, then you've arrived at the desired end goal: an example of a good partnership for your children to learn from. Amalia's parents divorced when she was four, and she thinks she has one of the happiest families around. But even in this best-case scenario, divorce doesn't occur in a vacuum. Another friend of ours—whose parents have been divorced since before she can remember—says, "It's not that divorce was a blight on my life. I've always thought my 'broken family' was a lot cheerier than most intact ones, with Mom, Dad, and Stepmom always happy to gather around the same table for the most minor of holidays. But a divorce implies there was once a choice made that might have been wrong, and the idea that a choice *could* be wrong is one that haunts choisters who are born with a desire to get it all right." Jennifer M., twenty-nine, says, "Watching my mom go through a two-year divorce has been awful. So as much as I want a partner, I might never get married purely because I never want to get divorced."

Caitlin T.'s divorced mother once said to her, "You'll do it better than I did." Her mom meant well—if anything, she wanted to calm any fears Caitlin might have of repeating her mother's mistakes—but it only added to the pressure her daughter already felt. After all, our parents grew up under a 5–8 percent divorce rate in the '50s and '60s, and they went on to failed attempts nearly half the time.[16] Based on those numbers, our own generation's chances look dismal. After surveying the world around us, we know we have to be incredibly lucky or unbelievably thorough in our prep work to beat the odds.

Of course, of the 50 percent of parents that didn't get divorced, we're not willing to say 100 percent were blissful. When we asked Mary M. what the primary difference would be between her marriage and the marriage of her parents, she answered, "I hope I love my partner, that we are equals, and that if things don't work out we divorce instead of white-knuckling our way through life." Well, that sounds sufficiently unpleasant. On a more tepid note, Sally S., twenty-five, claims: "My parents are still together and have been together thirty-six years, but I don't think that they are in love necessarily. They're comfortable, and they're fine, and it's easy for them."

And then there's the other, cheerier side of the coin, where your parents' marriage is so awesome you're convinced you need to hunt down its equal. Like Jenne L., twenty-eight, who says she "would love to have the kind of relationship that [her] parents have." Angelica S., a lawyer, feels the same: "My parents are the most fun, loving, hardworking people I know. And they're so good together. If I could have what they have, it'd be amazing." Liza G. remembers working on a paper in high school late one night, and at three o'clock overhearing her parents talking in their bedroom. The next morning she asked, "What were you guys doing up at that hour?" and they said, "We just woke up accidentally and then couldn't stop talking. We just kept thinking of more things we wanted to say to each other." Couldn't stop talking. After twenty years of marriage. Hats off to you two.

Now marriages have been successful and unsuccessful since the institution was invented, but rarely have kids taken such good notes on the state of their parents' union. There has been a lot of veil-piercing over the last thirty years about what goes into a marriage—there are the self-help books, the shocking nature and number of confessions on *Dr. Phil,* the divorced mothers—and together these have helped us shift from thinking it's none of our business to feeling that our parents' unions are there for us to study. Danika R., a twenty-seven-year-old student, observes of her mom and dad's marriage, "They lacked sexual chemistry and any kind of sexual freedom and physical affection." Anna M., twenty-two, thinks her parents would have had more respect for each other if not for "a language barrier," and Maria T. says, "My parents worked hard to make their marriage work, and while neither of them would deny that sometimes divorce is the best option for a couple, I think they place a high premium on fidelity."

As choisters, we watched, eavesdropped on, and dissected our parents' relationships with alarming depth. Linda B. still remembers the day her parents stopped kissing each other goodbye at the door. Jess H. can tell you about every twist and turn in her parents' three-year legal drama. And Cindy J. can tell that her mom really loves it when her dad jokes about his being jealous, even if it doesn't happen that often. When talking about her understanding of her parents' divorce, Erica L. says, "I try to put myself in my parents' shoes and the different ways they grew up and the different loves that they were taught." There was *never* an episode where Wally Cleaver did that.

Before the mass movement toward therapists, marriages were usually either "good" or "bad." Choisters have a more nuanced take on the situation, which inspires a whole new litany of projections for our own unions. Ah, the dangers of paying attention.

BESIDES LOVE

Clearly, we were absorbent little sponges as children, and the lessons did not stop with what to look for in a spouse. At home and at work, Mom and Dad showed us they believed in pursuing that which made them happy, so work was more than just a paycheck. When you pair that type of model with our parents' lifelong focus on our achievement, we know we would be simply disappointing them if we didn't look for the best—and only the best—in our own careers.

Thirty-plus years into the working world, our parents have achieved the goal of their generation to find not only a nice retirement package but also a reasonably fulfilling job they enjoy. Meg R., twenty-seven, says: "Not only is no one telling us to get a MRS degree, we're told 'It's not worth working if you're not passionate about what you do.'"

After all, our parents (and especially our mothers) were among the first generation to choose their careers with such flexibility, and we watched them choose work, love work, and slave over work all our lives. And nowadays, without children underfoot and bosses needing to be sucked up to, they've picked up . . . wait for it . . . legitimate hobbies. Travel junkies, marathon runners, students of various offbeat Slavic languages, members of book clubs, hospital volunteers—they have *lives*. Indeed, many of us want that life instead of our own student-loaned mess.

Think about it: By the time we graduated from liberal arts colleges with no tangible skills to speak of, our parents were professionally peaking. Long gone from the collective family memory are the multiple dinners of beans and rice that sustained us while a parent attended night classes or engaged in fights with the PhD committee. The days of professional and fiscal uncertainty are over, and the times of picking up the scut work their superiors did not want are in the past.

The fact that this is what we choisters see as we enter the work world understandably makes us examine our entry-level position with more skepticism than blind gratitude. When you compare your parents' well-paying jobs, comfortable homes, and hobby-filled lives with your own ramen-eating, futon-sleeping, no-time-to-IM-because-your-boss-needs-a-double-latte life—well, it's clear who is winning the imaginary rat race. But in their success, our parents provide the tempting carrot that can keep us rats running. We see not only the promise of eventual financial security but also a path toward that security that is enjoyed, not endured. We don't grow up thinking we need the money *or* the fulfillment—many of our parents show us that in time we could have both.

Our parents had plenty of professional issues, but at least they gave us a template on how to approach work that isn't too far off from what we end up wanting—money in addition to fulfill-ment. Not that life is ever so clear-cut. After years of glorifying her mother's job as a Hollywood director, twenty-six-year-old Jackie D. didn't know how to recalibrate when her mother said, "Try to stay at home with your kids. That would be ideal." But what about all the glory? What about having it all? *I was ready to make sacrifices for work,* thought Jackie, *and you're telling me work should be the sacrifice?*

We know it's a ridiculous exercise, but we can't help compar-ing our professional lives at twenty-seven to our parents' at fifty-five. Needless to say they don't match up. They may have loaned us a good template, but we'd like an advance on the lifestyle.

SO WHAT NOW?

An overwhelming majority—91 percent—of our generation reports a happy childhood; four in ten describe their childhood as being *very* happy.[17] And really everything that came after—our entire adulthood—is an attempt to keep hold of that happiness and not lose it. Never has a generation had the luxury of being so focused on joy. And it *is* a luxury. We cannot say enough times in this book how lucky we are for the lots we were given in life, and that includes the parents we have.

Whether it's by allowing us to live rent free in the family home after college, putting money toward our mostly unnecessary graduate school experiences, or prioritizing activities that cultivate personal enrichment, our parents have set us up to demand everything and never settle. With their safety net, too, many of us are staying put in choisterville, which is the only place it's encouraged for Lara to take drum lessons for one month at age twenty-six. By helping us, they're probably enabling us. But you know—in a constructive way. Really, don't stop.

It's not that they're quiet about their preference that we get on with it. We've heard the questions: Why don't you get your own place? Why don't you start thinking about settling down? How many more life experiences do you need? In response, we'd like to invoke a dramatic scene that has stayed with us since the days of our favorite antidrug ad: *We learned it from watching you, Dad.* (... and Mom.)

Our parents worked hard to find a unique balance between the practicality of their parents and their own. We don't agree with all they do or even want to copy their life path—but they do show

us that success and satisfaction don't have to be strange bedfellows in any area of life. Which is great to know as we go searching
for bedfellows of our own.

THE WORLD IS YOURS, CHOISTER

3

"Sell your script today!" "Looking for that Femme Fatale to add to our team!" "Take voice lessons to improve your chances on American Idol!" I scan the online ads and after a while am hit with information anxiety. There's too much to do, too much to be, and too much competition. So what do we do? How do we get off the hamster wheel? I'm sure an ad somewhere on my computer screen has the answer.

—KRISTEN R., AGE 25

So now we've waxed on (and on . . .) about choister childhoods and the unique expectations our parents tucked into our Jason Priestley backpacks before sending us off to synthesizer practice. But skip ahead a few years and suddenly our household exits were a bit more after-school special. It's a Saturday night, and we're asking the age-old "Don't you guys trust me?" as we try to shimmy out the door and over to Bobby's house. And our parents, true to form, claim, "Of course we trust *you*—we just don't trust the world." We realize now that was code for "No," but even in their faux reasoning they had a valid point: The world is a force to be reckoned with. Nowadays, we're (relatively) launched, and these fights have (generally) stopped, but we're still negotiating the tricky corners that our parents were so worried about. And let us tell you—it is a much wilder world than anyone realized.

Not that we're complaining! We've heard nothing but positive feedback from choisters about how remarkable and seemingly limitless this twenty-first century is. And we're uniquely qualified to opine on the state of that world because we're the ones in the best position to explore it, occupying as we do that particularly liberated period between being a kid and having a kid. A sampling of our immediate peer group reveals that choisters are banking in India, lawyering in Rome, consulting in Uganda, freelancing in Argentina, studying in California, and accomplishing impressive amounts from teeny tiny urban apartments everywhere. Clearly, we've inherited a world in which we're able to climb ladders and cross continents with new ease, which makes us increasingly hesitant to tie ourselves to one job, one location, and yes, one partner.

Look at us going on about options and freedom and euphoria. It must sound like we're trying to call bullshit on the largest economic convulsion of modern history with all this talk of opportunity and things being easier. We're not. We read the newspapers every day, we see our wages cut, but we've been told the world is ours to have for a lifetime—so we'll still get all we can out of it. Even if Amalia has just been told her writing assignments have been reduced by 50 percent for the next fiscal year, that won't stop her from doing the remaining work in London. She'll just use tea bags twice in a row and try to walk everywhere. Economically healthy or not, the world has shrunk. And by that we mean you can listen to Los Angeles radio stations online in Beirut and Skype with a friend in Japan from a Wifi-equipped bus driving through Ireland. Technology is opening doors at a faster rate than the financial world is closing them.

But if the world is at your fingertips, how do you hold hands with Bobby?

Turns out, you don't.

OH, THE PLACES WE'VE BEEN

The world may be smaller, but our frequent-flier accounts are undoubtedly bigger than ever before. According to a survey released by the Institute of International Education, students studying abroad increased by 144 percent in the last decade, from 84,403 in 1994 to 241,791 in 2006.[1] And this is only school-sponsored sojourns. After college, many twentysomethings will spend at least a few months abroad. As our survey showed, 60 percent of choisters living in the United States believe that travel plays a big role in their future plans and consider it a priority "to find a career/relationship that takes [them] abroad frequently." At our own college reunion, we learned that studying overseas was the one thing people in our class most regretted not doing.

Our diaries, kitchen walls, and blogs are filled with maps pin-pointing the cities we've traveled to. Cocktail parties are chock-full of "Where have you been recentlys?" and all conversation topics lead back to casual mentions of the strangest places no one else will have visited. One hot-as-hell day in Beijing, Claire literally walked *into* a tall white guy she had gone to college with, while Lara did her bizarre grade-school run-in over Mexican food in Mongolia. In what world does that happen? Ah yes, one in which there are over sixty applications on Facebook in the travel category, including "Where I've Been," which allows users—and there are reportedly 1.2 million—to mark where they've been, where they are, and where they want to go on a world map. We always have a half-packed suitcase standing by, know the loopholes of Southwest's Rapid Rewards program, and prep for our meetings on computers plugged into seat-side sockets. We know which airports have the best areas for snoozing and which airlines allow for free boozing.[2] Indeed, we fly across the world like we take a taxi across town. Amalia looks forward to the halfway mark each month when the movie lists on flights switch up, and Claire knows how to sweet-talk her oversize, face-wash-stuffed bag onto closed airport runways. Lara has added new visa pages again and again—a testament to both her extensive traveling and passport agents' inability to stamp pages in a space-efficient manner. And what's interesting here is that we're entirely unremarkable. None of us is the most well-traveled people we know.

And if you're not traveling now—because you have a "real" job—then you probably have traveled extensively in the past or have plans to travel in the near future. How many twentysome-things do you know who are already scheming how to cram all of

Latin America into a two-month hiatus from employment? And graduate school is a great excuse to get abroad. We know more than one choister who finally decided to return to academia *because* it would create an artificial summer in which to travel. "It's okay, Dad, I'm allowed to spend five months in Japan 'cause I'm going to law school in October." Anything to make it kosher.

It's not that we're some amazing new set of adventurers going where no woman has gone before. It's just damn easier to fly these days. While our parents were the first generation to grow up with access to commercial airlines, we are the first to really use and abuse it.[2] By the time you get to college, pretty much everyone has been on a plane, and it's a rarity to meet someone of the choister persuasion who hasn't left the country. A few years ago, it occurred to us that we didn't understand how people actually booked tickets in the precomputer days. No seriously—how did airlines get the passenger lists, and how did people pay for their tickets? Via postal mail? What the hell?

This light-in-the-heel lifestyle takes only two clicks to reserve and purchase, and it's also considerably, reliably cheaper. These days, you can fly from Los Angeles to San Francisco for $49 and roundtrip from L.A. to London for 50,000 frequent-flier miles. Gen Y-ers are the most profitable group for the airline biz precisely because we know about all these deals and we take advantage of them extremely regularly.[3] In 2009, European discount airline Ryanair started polling its passengers on whether or not they would be willing to stand on one-hour flights (yes, *stand*) if it meant they could fly for free. At first, Amalia balked at the idea and then marked the "yes" box. It appears we've turned some insane "travel or bust" corner.

And before some Baby Boomer scoffs at our jet-setting ways and makes some comment about trust funds or irresponsibility, know that choisters travel not because we are avoiding work (well, sometimes), but because a lot of times we've invented new, awesome ways to work while we travel. The multinational corporation has boomed in the last twenty years, and most people can enjoy the benefits of an exotically located office even within the cush of their staid investment job. There's also greater flexibility now that the Internet is in full swing—telecommuting is common, easy, and available, and more and more of us are doing it.[4]

Consider yours truly. While authoring this book, there have been other jobs we've pieced together to pay the bills: editing essays, launching financial advice blogs, checking for "porn" matches online for nanny-bots, and doing PR for maternity clothing lines—all with out-of-country status. Although it wasn't the most cohesive, enjoyable, graduate-application-friendly career strategy, it did make that trip through East Asia possible.

Travel carries such a premium that even when we don't actually have the funds to do it, we'll still do it. Take Casey Fenton, age thirty, founder of CouchSurfing.org. The idea for the site arose after Fenton, who'd traveled to Iceland on a last-minute cheap flight, emailed 1,500 students from the University of Iceland asking if he could stay at one of their places because he didn't want to pay for a hostel. He received over fifty offers, and the strangest of start-ups was born. As of August 2009, CouchSurfing.org has well over 1,200,000 members from around the world, and according to Alexa. com it's the most visited hospitality service on the Internet.[5] Yet again, choisters are using technology to find ways around financial roadblocks.

LOVE 'EM WHILE LEAVING 'EM

So how does the fact that Claire spends one out of every thirty-six hours on a plane affect her romantic life? For starters, travel puts life at home on a timeout. Which is fine if you're permitted a meager ten vacation days per year, but problematic when you're supposed to be managing client expectations in Tokyo every other month. That's a lot of life on hold, and a lot of time spent away from a relationship.

When you're trying to calculate the disruptiveness of a jog in the middle of your day, you have to take into account so much more than the thirty minutes you're actually huffing and puffing. There's the stretching beforehand and the showering and self-congratulating afterward. Travel's the same. A five-day trip is at least seven days away from normal life, with all the compressing and decompressing. It's exhausting, and the last thing you want to do is end up in a serious relationship talk—instead, you'd rather sit on the couch in your Juicy Couture tracksuit and watch telenovelas in a jet-lagged haze.

When it comes to dating, this tension is certainly something our generation is feeling: Our survey says the majority of us have had a relationship strained by distance—and not because of concerns over infidelity. People's main problem with long-distance was the way it stunted a couple's growth. A relationship needs energy and attention if it's going to move forward. And if you're always packing for your next business trip or recovering from your last one, it's hard to muster up the energy to care that Johnny's feeling stressed. But it does make it easier to find Johnny's knuckle-cracking habit more tolerable—turns out everything's adorable when glazed over by a grateful-to-finally-have-physical-contact-again fog. Such fogs have an expiration date of about five days—after which point plenty of long-distance choisters are back out the door. Is that relationship growing? Not really, no. It's just sort of . . . stuck.

The other problem for a relationship is what happens at the other end of the flight—whether traveling for work or recreation, choisters are falling in love with more destinations and imagining what their life could look like if it happened in front of a different backdrop or in a different language. Suddenly home's not a haven, it's a holding cell, and your relationship gets either a new shot of distance or a new source of strain. Of course, there is also the potential of exotic hookups to dissuade us from signing up for that long-distance relationship, and according to our polls, the tempting ass of those exotic fruits has been bitten by a surprising number of our peers.

There's certainly a case to be made that we travel more because we're not married, but are we not married *because* we travel more? It's hard to invest in someone when you only see them in four-day spurts, and harder still to remember how great you are together when you suddenly realize there's been a horrible error and you were supposed to have been born in Mexico (the margaritas, the mariachi, the musky men—it's all working for you).

And beyond the convenience, why do choisters travel? As the fifth-century theologian St. Augustine said, "The world is a book and those who do not travel read only one page."[6] Deep. Wanderlust is not unique to our generation, and it's not a frivolous, youthful urge. In an interview with Bookreporter.com, *Eat, Pray, Love* author Elizabeth Gilbert talks about the timeless, universal appeal of travel. "Humans spent a whole lot of time wandering and seeking and exploring this world (and themselves within it) long before there ever was such a thing as America," she says.[7]

Travel carries value for our generation, and it becomes the venture we invest our capital in. But the travel bug isn't the only thing we have infecting our choister systems. In business class, or in your pajamas, there's one denominator we have in common after college: work. And the endless death match between professional and personal commitments is going full throttle.

HI, HO! IT'S OFF TO WORK WE GO

You already know there's an inverse relationship between your work and love life. You know it every time you make the choice to appease your boss, who's asking for edits to that Excel spreadsheet, and end up sending your boyfriend a lame "I'm sorry" text with five emoticons. You know it when you move across the country for a promotion and willingly sign up for a year of mediocre phone sex with your man (thank God for video chat). Or, if you *don't* move for that promotion, you *really* know it as you lie awake next to him and think about when exactly you became your mother. When we talked to choisters about romance, every single person—100 percent—said work was the main competitor for their attention, whereas only a measly 15 percent of those people said their boyfriend was their main time suck.

Take it from twenty-nine-year-old PR professional Delilah R.: "Right now, I am dating someone and starting to see him on a regular basis, but I don't feel like I can be seriously involved because work is insane. I can barely return personal emails these days, let alone manage a relationship through those shaky first six months." Shana W., twenty-seven, discusses her hesitations surrounding marriage as primarily stemming from work. "I think I'll feel more 'ready' to get married when I have a slightly clearer sense of who/where I want to be professionally and have the pieces in place to make that happen." It's a legitimate problem. When someone asks you about yourself, you'll either tell them what you do *or* who you're doing. And if you're an ambitious, career-minded woman like Delilah or Shana, the "what" might feel more defining than the "who."

For women, this newly enhanced focus on work certainly has a great deal to do with the professional ceilings we've broken through. According to the United States Department of Labor, women currently make up about 48 percent of the labor force while men represent 52 percent, a change from the 1988 statistics of 45 and 55 percent, respectively.[8] Today, there are 9.1 million women-owned businesses in the United States, representing nearly 40 percent of all businesses; they employ 27.5 million people and generate more than $3.6 trillion in sales (surprisingly, it's *not* all Oprah).[9] Suddenly, the classic scene of a frustrated spouse waiting at home as the pork chops get cold does not necessarily star a woman anymore.

Kristen R., twenty-five, reflects on the generational shift: "When I was little, Mom made tuna casserole and Dad came home from work every day carrying a hard leather briefcase. The day my little sister learned to walk, she picked up a Nike shoebox with a handle on it and headed for the door. Twenty years later, the briefcases are gone, and the women of today are picking up their iPhones and walking."[10]

Work is a major distraction from all things romantic not only because we, as women, are able to do more of it but also because our generation has different expectations of its work life. Traditionally, "work" is supposed to be a means to a financial end. You know, so that there's food on the table? But choisters have something different in mind. As discussed in Chapter 2, we like our happiness and were raised to keep a close eye on it, making sure it never got too far out of reach. With the equation burned into our minds from a young age that accomplishment should equal fulfillment, we have a hard time staying in the role of "coffee fetcher and copy maker" for very long. In the words of Meg R., "My father just told me that money doesn't matter—nothing matters except loving your life and loving what you do." Great. We did not love making copies.

And the same sense of entitlement that motivates you to quit your job after three months because you don't like the bitch work also tends to lead you toward tangential activities like serving on a kibbutz in Israel (and suddenly we're back to the travel). Conveniently, kibbutzim have recently changed their slogan, "From each according to his ability, to each according to his needs" to "From each according to his *preferences*, to each according to his needs."[11] Way to keep with the times 'buttzie—keep us happy and no one will realize they're schlepping mangos all day.

But now we're getting into dangerous, self-deprecating territory, because behind the attitude lies the truth that choisters work devilishly hard. We realize that there is ladder climbing to be done and the bottom rungs will be grimy. It's not that we're unwilling to push paper, we just have to know and want what comes next. Because corporate ascent is not rewarding enough, we need something more than an annual lift in earnings or rank. As Sophie W. explains it: "I think I'd be fine with having a consuming job as long as it's one where I feel a bit more of a personal "return"—i.e., putting the time and energy into a cause/company/industry I really believe in and can get genuinely excited about. I do think that in this day and age it's human nature to feel a bit frustrated that you don't have time to do everything you want. I wonder if that feeling subsides as you mature?"

Probably not. But keep your chin up, girlie.

Choisters gravitate to careers that either make you happy or allow you the time to explore things that do. If your entry-level job doesn't thrill you, then at least you should be able to get off by six-thirty every day and fit in hours of mountain biking. It's a noted trend in the workplace that Generation Y has very different demands than its Baby Boomer bosses. Many of us are exiting the workplace, in fact, and making a living with jobs like professional blogger (all flexibility, little subordination) and everything else author Tim Ferriss tells us to do in his book *The 4-Hour Workweek*. As Michael S. Malone wrote in his May 2008 essay, "The Next American Frontier," ours has become "a nation in which the dominant paradigm is entrepreneurship . . . entire careers built on perpetual change, independence and the endless pursuit of the next opportunity."[12] That's just the choister definition put into business-speak.

What better metaphor for this professional restlessness than San Francisco's explosion of street food-carts, staffed by a combination of chefs who want to serve great food without the hassle of manning a full-service restaurant and foodies who'd rather cook up curry than return to a desk job. There's the Crème Brûlée cart, the Amuse Bouche cart, and the Urban Nectar cart that sells fresh-squeezed watermelon and strawberry juice. Or Spencer on the Go, which serves fine French cuisine from a converted taco truck.

Hovering over tiny burners in the cold, these groups find the free-dom to do what they want how they want. "Fun-employed" was the term used by a laid-off marketing executive, featured in the *San Francisco Chronicle,* who sells barbeque pork sandwiches from dif-ferent Mission bars.[13]

Aside from being financially viable, we should leave our desks feeling intellectually satisfied, good about ourselves, and enter-tained. With those qualifiers, work starts to sound like our relation-ships. The problem with this is that when love and work are feed-ing the same parts of your psyche, they become direct competitors. Sure, relationships give you those physical and emotional perks, but most offices have cereal-stocked kitchens.

Caroline B., a twenty-six-year-old law student, feels that same tension: "I get stressed about my relationship distracting me from and lessening my chances of success professionally. I'm trying to get things off the ground, so I see my mid- and late twenties as a time that requires serious focus." Gone are the days of working for a single company your entire life, and in their place are nights spent strategizing job changes. What was once a decision expected to last until retirement now expires in two to three years. Which means we spend a lot of time thinking about work, strategizing about work, and making pro/con lists about work.[14]

It's a consuming relationship we have with our careers. Not to mention our demanding bosses, who are the human equivalent of our insanely heavy elementary school backpacks. An embarrassing number of us pop into the office on Saturdays and sleep within arm's reach of our BlackBerry. About two-thirds eat lunch at their desks, according to a survey by the American Dietetic Association.[15] And it continues to baffle these authors why rush hour happens between four and six in the evening when we don't know a single person who leaves work before seven. And for those hours you're *not* in the office, email and cell phones keep you on deck. With all the pinging from your iPhone Tweetie app, how's a lover supposed to get a word (let alone a romantic night—wink, wink) in edgewise? In competition, work plays nasty.

Once upon a time, we thought we could be supergirlfriend and superemployee. And then the clock struck midnight and we realized twenty-four hours in a day is not enough time to get both glass slippers on. As Simone G., twenty-six, says, "The faster you go at work, the slower you move on all other fronts." Every new deadline means a bill you'll forget to pay and a relationship you'll either take too long to get out of or simply never get to start. And as far as marriage and children are concerned, it's much harder to worry about a reproductive timeline when work deadlines are just so much more imminent. Who has the time to stomp their feet about biological clocks ticking, à la Marisa Tomei in *My Cousin Vinny*, when they're racing off to an 8:00 AM meeting?

SCIENCE: NOT AS USELESS AS WE THOUGHT

Perhaps just as potent an influence on our romantic decisions— or inability to make them—is science. Even if we don't (care to) understand what happens behind laboratory doors, we're grateful to those goggled people who increased our control over when we have children. After all, we wouldn't be jetting off around the world or working late at the office if science hadn't given us the power to put off pregnancy till a date more convenient than nine months after hubby decides he's feeling extra sexy one night. As Bea Campbell, the feminist academic and writer, said, "For as long as women have been bearing children they have been fighting for control over *how* and *when* they have children."[16]

In a book about choices, we would be remiss not to mention the birth control menu. In addition to the old standbys—the Pill, condoms, and diaphragms—we choisters have a plethora of options to choose from, including three faves: Implanon, Depo-Provera, and the Ring. With so many ways to have sex without babies, it seems a downright waste *not* to have casual (protected!) sex. At least some choisters are of that mind. The absence of babies—no matter how much we may want them *some*day—means we can focus on our careers and flit around from one potential mate to the next. Pills that we began taking to clear up our teenage acne or regulate our temperamental periods are now tickets to *riiiide,* baby. Of those women on birth control (61.9 percent), more use the Pill (19.2 percent) than any other method.[17] And unlike the diaphragm, whose bothersome insertion process might have once acted as an obstacle, the Pill tempts any girl to tell her tired boyfriend, "I've fucking remembered to take these pills for the last week, so you *better* have sex with me tonight." Sexy.

And then there's that other pill. The one that comes with all the politics. In the last few years, Plan B has gone from something a doctor had to prescribe to something a Walgreens employee tosses at you from behind the counter. ("Do you have any questio—?" "No.") Soon they'll be dispensed by vending machines in ladies bathrooms everywhere. Say what you will about it, but Plan B's availability is liberating the female psyche. We're not dismissing accountability, but there's no question that medical advancements have unhitched women from the baby wagon. And with all this emphasis on avoiding it, one can't help but feel like the baby wagon is the one to fall off of.

If having a baby decides a lot about what the next twenty years will look like, then taking birth control allows you to keep life undecided. And taking birth control not only means you can avoid having a baby with boyfriend #3, it also allows a certain sexual license because it strips the act of much (if not most) consequence. Birth control also has an effect on women's mind-set by giving them increased say in their futures. The founder of what would become Planned Parenthood, Margaret Sanger, said in 1920, "No woman can call herself free until she can choose consciously whether she will or will not be a mother."[18] And feeling free can make us feisty.

It's all interconnected. The increase in female participation in the workforce has strong ties to birth control (go, Ortho Tri-Cyclen, go!) and advances in fertility treatments. Fewer unplanned or impossible pregnancies means increased control over one's career path; and isn't the corporate ladder more tempting if you can be sure you won't be knocked off by a surprising pink plus sign? In the words of Elizabeth B., twenty-seven, "My anxiety about children centers on my career. My hope is that by the time I'm ready to have kids I will have a job that will make the transition easier. Then again, the entire idea of childbirth and childrearing scares the shit out of me, so I'm not really in any rush."

In sum, birth control has (mostly) done away with shotgun weddings, and the promise of delayed fertility has helped us all hunker down in a diaper-free zone. At least, that is, until we decide to follow that trail of pills right back toward fertility.

ONE ORDER OF BABY

Scientific strides have upgraded women's pool of choice from wading to Olympic size. Now we can take our birth control cocktail until the age of thirty-nine if we want, because there's a new bevy of pills and injections to pump into our bodies once we get there—this time in hopes of *having* a baby. Fertility medicine has made huge steps forward in the last twenty years, and the pace of change has increased dramatically in just the last few. When the time is "right," choisters get to choose between fertility drugs, artificial insemination, surgery, in vitro fertilization (IVF), surrogacy, and egg donors.

And for many, these are very attractive options. Meg R., twenty-nine, tells us, "After college, I was in a relationship with a woman for three years. Ultimately it didn't work out, but it did get me thinking about alternative paths to having kids. I was twenty-five and about to go to medical school, and I thought, *If I'm not with the person I want to be with by the time I'm thirty-five, I'll just do it on my own."*

While the body has predetermined "windows of opportunity," advancements in medicine have budged that window up the hill of aging. It's a rickety new frame, but there's often enough space to pass a baby through. Maria T., twenty-eight, would like to have babies before she's thirty-five. "But things like personal health and career goals," she says, "seem just as important as having kids right now."

And we have multiple examples of people who are putting off childbearing, or already planning their what-if scenarios. Simply look at the always-copyable lives of celebrities like Courteney Cox, Marcia Cross, and Brooke Shields. As they're some of the most beautiful, impregnable women in the world, is it not relieving that they waited until they were over the age of thirty-five to conceive? All three have been public in saying that fertility treatments played a role in their baby plan, and many of the choisters we talked to said that such public profiles helped them begin to understand their own lifestyle options.

Of course, most of us are still a few years away from such dilemmas. The majority won't be turning to fertility treatments until we're at least in our late thirties, which puts us past the peak of choister romantic indecision. So what does the existence of such scientific advancements mean to our present life? It's all about safety nets. Knowing that we can fall back on IVF lets us feel more comfortable about dating the not-marriage-material boy toy, or using our twenty-sixth year around the sun to explore Buddhism instead of Bill and baby bottles. With fertility treatments at your disposal, you can search for Mr. Right that much longer. Or, if you don't find him, you're a big girl, and you've got other ways to get bigger all by yourself.

And there's always the Jolie-Pitt route. Shana W., twenty-seven, sums it up well: "I feel like I might be more likely to adopt if I were forty-four and unmarried, rather than settle." And Shana's not alone. Choisters everywhere seem to think that choosing your own way is the only good way these days.

THE INTERNETS

In the exploration of lifestyle options, let us now turn to another overly broad topic: technology. The fact that the larger world feels smaller (Skyping to your boyfriend in Hong Kong does that to you) often makes an individual's world seem bigger (having a boyfriend in Hong Kong whom you can Skype with in the first place). In truth, the Internet is the extra battery energizing the above-mentioned progress in travel, career, and science. With the advent of the web, the world is almost within arm's length. No, make that a finger's length (Click! Send! Call! Apply!).

Thanks to Craigslist, which has added the qualifier *telecommute* to its short list of advanced options, you can find a graphic design job that pays New York rates while you live in Timbuktu at decidedly less than New York prices. Claire and Lara managed to spend a year traveling around the world, not because their parents bequeathed them any money, but because they wiled their way into awesome (read: boring but profitable) online jobs. Amalia went on one of those nifty Israel birthright trips and was able to write articles from a basement computer cluster in her Jerusalem hostel. The global reality is that in many parts of the world, crappy hourly wages in USD can get you pretty far.

Not only has technology made it easier to telecommute to your job, it's created an entirely new league of professionals. Since the Internet gained traction, thousands of jobs have emerged that simply never existed before: Java developer, Internet marketing specialist, webmaster (so wizardy!), database analyst, user-interface designer, SEO writer, and on and on. All this work really does translate into more brilliance from pajamas. At least for Lara and Amalia. Claire read an article somewhere that claims getting dressed (with shoes!) every morning will help you be more productive in your day. This translates to Claire sitting at her laptop by 8:00 AM every morning with heels on even if she doesn't leave the house (or her seat) for the next eight hours. It's so hard not to mock her earnestness.

But back to task. The Internet really does encourage our need for instant gratification and confirms the "anything is possible" ideal we grew up with. With all the hundreds of gadgets you're carrying around with you, who *can't* handle a crisis? In our favorite example, our two friends got married in an extraordinarily well-planned wedding only to find themselves in the car outside the reception, exhausted, without directions to their hotel and only an iPhone to guide them through. "This should be an iPhone commercial," said the bride with the gadget. In our information world, there's no need to spend time planning ahead. No need to print confirmation codes when you can just pull it up on your Mac at the ticket window. You can notify credit cards about international usage while waiting to board.

Amalia was on a five-hour bus ride in the British countryside recently when she suddenly remembered that it was her mother's birthday. Lucky for her, the bus had a free wireless Internet connection. Her mother was so bedazzled by Amalia's Skyping powers that she didn't even remember there were only two minutes left to her birthday and that her firstborn had nearly missed it. You may have heard the wise adage "There are very few problems money can't solve." We'd like to posit there are very few problems the Internet can't solve.

But it's almost like the human race wasn't built to spend twenty hours a day in front of illuminated screens. With fifty Firefox tabs open at any given time, we're like little kids on a sugar high with five more milkshakes in front of us. When everything is online, what whim don't you indulge? And suddenly we end up checking out streaming videos of puppies (Amalia), a million pictures of Zahara Jolie-Pitt (Claire), and clothes we'll covet for their beauty and berate for their expense (Lara). The nature of the computer is that there is no commitment. No one even has to know what you were just looking at—we erased the history! We can't even fathom banging out a paper on a typewriter. Amalia cops to having been working on a painting recently and having the impulse to hit Ctrl+Z when she made a mistake. Pity her.

Oh yes, which brings us to the matter of social networking sites. Oh social networking—you harsh mistress, you. Here again is an example of technology making the world at large feel small, and thereby broadening our bubble. So how—besides wasting precious baby-making hours by looking through Halloween photos—does Facebook keep your options open? Well, when you can track the day-to-day whereabouts of your high school crush, it's not *awesome* for your current relationship.

Thirty years ago, the people you interacted with included your man, the couple of friends you phoned regularly, and the person at the desk next to yours. That's at most a handful of people. Now you're unpopular if you get only twenty emails in an hour and have a meager two hundred friends on Facebook. And the more members of the opposite sex you're in touch with, the harder it is to, in the dismal words of Crosby, Stills, Nash & Young, "love the one you're with." Sarah L. is a stay-at-home writer, which means she wears pajamas 24/7 and the only person she interacts with during the day before her boyfriend comes home is her mother over AIM. Given these nunnish circumstances, you'd think she'd rarely be tempted to stray. But with the magic of Facebook and other sites, Sarah's old exes, high school boyfriends, and various other ghosts from her past just might rise from the dead.

But folks beware—what happens on Facebook doesn't stay on Facebook. Ruby K. gives an example: "Both my mom and my ex's mom found out about the breakup through Facebook, and both called demanding answers. The interesting thing to me is that

I didn't really advertise the breakup on Facebook at all—I simply changed my relationship status and BAM! Flooded."[19] Clearly, everyone's trolling the Internet. And let's just say it can be a bit hard to focus on what your boyfriend is saying when your high school football team has just "poked" you.

WRAP IT UP, LADIES

In the new millennium, there are infinitely more directions to take life in, more choices that make it harder to commit to just one partner. As Lucy M. points out, "I think there are times in your life when it's time to focus on yourself, your career, your family, your friends, your community, your health, your future, or any combination of these things. To add a mate into the mix is a whole other bag of tricks." Paired with our innate reluctance to choose, every option gets more glittery.

Ask Jenny S. about how she balances all the opportunities around her. "I feel distracted by all the things I could be doing every single day. I could be volunteering, I could be traveling, I could be taking vacations, I could be in a serious relationship, I could be applying myself more to my career, I could be going out more instead of working late, I could be a better friend, I could be at the gym tonight. There are a million of these thoughts that go through my head on a daily basis, to the point where it is so overwhelming that I feel paralyzed and do none of it. I feel immense pressure to be more accomplished by thirty than I am, and I have a lot of self-loathing about that."

And at a time when our expectations for romantic relationships are on the up and up, the world of options makes holding off on marriage much easier. But it doesn't mean you *have* to take advantage of every opportunity. While Claire and Lara were tracking their travels around the world on their blog, TrippingOnWords, Amalia set up a sister site appropriately titled TrippingOnMyCouch in San Francisco, where she took pictures of herself in pajamas next to green plants with signs reading I AM IN GUATEMALA. Not only do all these new choices sometimes replace our choosing a significant other but they also, at the very least, turn us into dizzied people too busy to settle down. But who says that's bad? Shouldn't we applaud Renaissance woman Caroline B. when she says: "I want to travel and see the world, I want to launch a business, earn an income, write a movie script, fall in love, take dance classes and guitar classes, learn to cook well, and be a liberated businesswoman."

Advancements in the world—produced in medical labs or Washington marches—have expanded our selection of choices and made it all too easy to veer off the trail our parents blazed for us. It's like being a kid in a candy store—except you're allowed to taste *everything*. Somehow we've all become like Claire on her first day in a college dining hall (we promise this story is true), when she piled her tray high and then looked over at the football players' and asked, "Is that ALL you're eating?"

THE CHOISTERS COMETH

4

I roll my eyes at college dating. College is the place where you should learn how to date and communicate, and instead we learn how to write a blasé email asking someone to a sorority party, where we then get smashed and "see how things develop."

—ANGELICA S., AGE 28

Amalia is the nostalgic one of us, and she likes to reminisce. Particularly as far back as the day when she first tried to explain the concept of this book to her mother. "We're a whole new generation!" she cried. Her mother did not look convinced. "We have all these new realities we're facing!" Amalia trilled. " . . . and we date around, and we don't want our parents' marriages . . . " Her mother gently interrupted, "We did that too." As if Amalia's generation were simply retracing the path already stomped out by Baby Boomers. Amalia started to panic inside—oh god, what are we going to write about—and then she asked her mother if she'd ever wanted to be single. And something clicked. For all her independent, free-spirited ways, Amalia's mother never actually *wanted* to be single as a young woman. She may have wanted to be with someone other than the person she was with, but she never particularly wanted to be unpartnered for any real length of time. Point: choister.

Things are different now, as evidenced by the rise of online dating, speed-dating, and the fact that shows like the Bachelor Millionaire's Real Chance at a Big Fat Fiancé never end up with a wedding. Apparently, when it comes to exploring the choister lifestyle distractions, the single life provides the perfect vantage point. Today's young women seem to view being boyfriendless as more ripe opportunity than lonely wasteland.

But aren't the people who extol the virtues of single living just trying to cover up their loneliness? There must be some dark underbelly to the unmarrieds clinking mojitos throughout the city. Are singletons masking their pain when they travel solo to far-off lands, or when they stay in, get their favorite Chinese, and hiccupily sob through *The Notebook?*

Nope.

Although a stigma remains for the single gal, going solo doesn't mean going lonely. Meg R., twenty-nine, remembers her mother telling her that she "went to college in the '60s and stormed and marched on Washington, and yet on a Saturday night, if she didn't have a date, she felt embarrassed and would stay at home in her dorm room." As for Meg R. herself? "I did not live like that," she says. "That is not my reality."

For generations of women past, there has been little inherently attractive about being on your own. In 1957, a poll showed that "only 9 percent of Americans thought a single person could be happy."[1] In contrast, 77 percent of the choisters we surveyed look back on the single periods of their adult life as happy times, and 93 percent consider being single important to their personal maturation. We hardly claim that every woman to come before us in history only wanted a lifelong mate, and we're suddenly the first ones to say "I choose *me!*" (à la *90210*'s Kelly Taylor). But those who felt totally okay being alone in the past were an exception, not a rule. Today, it is so comfortable to be single that visions of the unattached lifestyle have begun haunting smug, monogrammed, and berobed couples everywhere.

Allow us to digress to a Theory We Have Already Introduced but Will Explore More Now: If ever there were an era to be single in, it's this one.

So live it up.

No, even more than that.

There's no doubt that opportunities for women increase exponentially with each new round of American bat mitzvahs, *quinceañeras*, and debutante balls. But what may not be as clear is the fact that advances for women are affecting the single ladies more than any other subset. (It's the least they're due after decades of having to tune out whispers of "spinster.")

Nowadays, women can buy a blinged out vibrator, travel on a whim to Jakarta without concern for anyone else's Google calendar, and work late and guilt free at the office if that's what it takes to get the promotion. There are so many options lying in wait for today's choister that the choice to compromise for another person leaves her more compromised than ever.

What's amazing about this day and age is that money, travel, friends, and career are not just the false deities that distract single choisters while they eat their feelings, women are happily adding value to their life and using their single powers for good.

YOUR LOVE WON'T PAY MY BILLS

There's a lot to being single in today's world, so let's get some of the business out of the way. Grandma may have taught us that money is a dirty word, but it's a reality we have to deal with so we can fully enjoy the dirtier stuff later (or you can just skip to page 91).

Women have always had a complicated relationship with men and money. From the days when a daughter was married off in exchange for a goat to the era when our mothers were told to keep their eyes peeled for a handsome doctor, women have been taught that their security is linked to the financial wherewithal of a spouse. But today's women are working and earning more, and the rules have changed accordingly. If a historic lack of financial independence compelled women to get married in the past, then the recent accrual of independence lets us stay single longer.

As Manisha Thakor, financial literacy advocate and author of *Get Financially Naked*, puts it, "When you are unmarried, you are in complete control of your budget. You set your standard of living. You decide whether to be more of a spender or a saver. When you are married, two different sets of values, histories, and beliefs about money come crashing together. In other words, when you marry someone, you marry their money history as well, and that union is often explosive."[2] No surprise there—we all know money (alongside sex and children) is the main contributor to divorce. Perhaps it's because of how cramped an oyster can get when you have to share its little shell with another person.

This potential conflict of financial values in a marriage is only increasing with each passing generation, as women start getting more literate in the tricky ways of Roth IRAs and retirement savings. While Claire's mom was one of only a handful of women in her MBA class, the percentage of women in Claire and Lara's MBA classes hovered between the now usual 25–35 percent (yep—battle isn't over in the MBA world, sisters).[3] Indeed, the number of women earning degrees in business, accounting, and all manner of finance *shminance* topics has risen dramatically in recent years, as has their enrollment in graduate schools in general.[4]

Women are buying homes, cars, and pets—without cosigning husbands or "Daddy knows bests"—with more regularity than ever. David Bach's *Smart Women Finish Rich* may not have hit such a chord were it published in 1960, but in this generation, its bestseller status was instant. Hundreds of thousands of copies quickly fell into the handbags of young women wanting to make their own economic and investment decisions. (An Amazon.com search for "finance" books published before 1980 gave an impressive 35,000-plus results. Books on "finance and women" before 1980? 135. Books on "finance and women" *since* 1980? Nearly 10,000.

Just sayin'.) And we all know that Suze Orman doesn't have a husband putting food on her dinner table—for many reasons, really. Nope, her bread comes from the millions of women happy to pay for financial advice. Women are hungry for fiscal know-how and scared of the alternative. Maria T., twenty-eight, says that her new husband is "more interested in financial investing than [she is]," but quickly expresses her concern that this imbalance will leave her "pregnant, barefoot, and ignorant in the kitchen" someday. Women today understand the power that comes with money, and we want more of it.

According to one survey, 49 percent of respondents "say retirement benefits are a very important factor in their job choices. Among those eligible, 70% of Gen Y . . . contribute to their 401(k) plan."[5] And this is all in addition to Math 101 for adults, i.e., taxes. Most of our grandmothers went from being a child dependent to being a dependent wife. So our mothers were the first generation to make a decent living on their own, building miniature savings accounts in their early twenties and declaring this brief financial independence on 1040s.

So having dipped their feet into the financial world, our mothers weren't scared to focus on raising daughters to be more than traditional housewives. After all, if little Sarah was going to go to the moon, she needed to be able to handle her paycheck back on Earth. When Mattel came out with one of the worst marketing blunders of the '90s, Teen Talk Barbie, who was programmed to say things like "Math class is tough!" and "Let's go shopping!" it didn't take long for modern moms to be up in arms. They did not look favorably upon a big-breasted plastic doll telling their daughters not to distract their pretty heads with numbers. After all, our mothers were arguably the first generation with a fair shot at bringing home some serious bacon, and many are still quite pleased with their success and eager to see their daughters go whole hog.

But it's not only pride prompting our mothers; it's protective mama bear instincts as well. Divorce often leaves financial ruin in its wake, and mothers try to arm their daughters with enough financial savvy to make them invulnerable to their spouse's whims (like gambling or the leggy new nanny). If a parents' divorce forces a kid to reflect on her parents' relationship (however much she'd like to ignore the issue), the matters of alimony and settlements make her think about money and strategy in a way unfamiliar to most. Diana J. watched her mother's divorce drain her of her retirement. "Not only from what my stepdad is taking and demanding," she says, "but from attorney's fees, and the back-and-forth and the fact that people get nastier and nastier the longer it goes on."

Clearly, for women today, home economics no longer means sewing on buttons and making apple crumble (to a fault, thinks Claire, who FedExes things to her grandmother to hem). It means greater financial savoir faire, which is intended to guarantee the freedom to make our own decisions. This combo of an independent mind and money in our pocket has meant we have the chance to choose exactly what we want and when we want it: two things that are crucial to being both single and a choister.

One of the choices young women are making more and more these days is to live alone, or with a gaggle of girlfriends. In 2005, 51 percent of women were living without a spouse, an increase from 35 percent in 1950 and 49 percent in 2000.[6] Most choisters agree that living independently is an integral part of the growing up process—it teaches you about bills, household chores, and navigating the chaotic early morning bathroom hour—all before you have to negotiate such corners with your life partner. But solo-dwelling isn't only instructive—it's liberating. Nothing is more personal and precious than your home, and being queen of even the tiniest domain can be addictive. Stacy S. R., twenty-five, predicts that even when she gets married in the future, she'll still try to carve out some space just for herself. "I'll always want at least a room that everyone else has to knock to come into," she says. "That's weirdly important."

A key factor in our enjoyment of living alone is that it is no longer socially taboo. No one looks at you askance or worries about your mental state when you announce your big solo moving day. Full independence seems to be a relative term, however, what with all those move-out dinner parties, housewarming dinner parties, and "I miss you" dinner parties.

THE RISE OF THE BFFS

These roommates in the postcollege years are just one of many varieties of the choister friend, and they're a small part of an ensemble cast that also stars college friend, high school friend, family friend, partying friend, etc. The list really does go on and on. This intensely meaningful support network is at the epicenter of the choister universe—single or not—and we choisters protect these bonds with all the power our little Tae-Bo-punching selves can muster. As the infamous Mr. Big said to Miranda, Charlotte, and Samantha in one scene of *Sex and the City*: "You're the loves of her life. A guy's just lucky to come in fourth." Granted, he was sucking up to the ladies at the time, but it's true: A romantic relationship is not the only way—or even the best way—to stave off loneliness. Thankfully, bands of BFFs are now giving boyfriends a run for their money when it comes to a choister's emotional and social fulfillment.

As Allison P., twenty-seven, says, "I can't imagine my life without my friends, whereas I feel like I would get by fine if I didn't have a boyfriend. In fact, I have. The first two relationships I had postcollege never progressed because I couldn't transition to being completely in a relationship. I was in the mind-set—'I want to go out with my girls tonight—why should I feel guilty?' Oh . . . right, because he wants to hang out, too."

We've already established that more of us are waiting longer to get married, and the impact of this on society is that single women are no longer the old maids in the corner; they *are* the corner, and the corner is threatening to blow up the room. Or something like that. What we're trying to say is that it's a better playground for singles, and there are more of us mud-wrestling in the sandbox.

Meg R., twenty-nine, attests: "My eighty-year-old therapist wants me to get married. She's totally the pressure I've never had. She'll ask about my weekend—'Did you meet a boy? Did you meet a boy?'—and then I respond with, 'I had the best weekend! I did this and that with my friends,' and she thinks I'm insanely involved with my girlfriends. It might be subconscious, but I think it's a defense mechanism because marriage isn't forever and *these* relationships *are* fucking forever." She continues, "And everything else can fall apart, and my life will still be interesting and fun because I have fucking fantastic friends to have fabulous dinners with, and it's always going to be okay."

As single women and their backup dancers take to the streets, the public is taking note. Look at author Sasha Cagen, who coined the phrase "quirkyalone" in her best-selling book by the same name. The term refers to "people who enjoy being single (but are not opposed to being in a relationship) and prefer being single to dating for the sake of being in a relationship."[7] Quirkyalones believe in a world in which you stay single until you have met someone amazing who truly completes you. Because what's the rush, when it ain't so bad being single in the first place? Until you find someone who thinks it's cool that you like to use a neti pot to clean out your nasal passages, you shouldn't have to compromise such uniquely you behavior! Quirkyalones and choisters *get* each other. After all, it is an inherently choister idea that you refuse to settle, and that you think you can have absolutely everything—the neti pot and the partner who can enjoy watching you do it. And if you don't have that magical alchemy of a combination? Then, love the single life you're with.

Although we are fully on board with a movement of single women, we have a linguistic bone to pick with the term "quirky-alone." Are they really all that *alone?* We say no, and we've got seven BFFs to prove it (we don't ever call them that). Even though women of our generation may be living independently, this doesn't mean that they don't have a full dance card. It just happens to prominently feature names like "Lana" and "Christina" on it instead of "Joey" and "Hans." And the type of dancing is a little bit different—less Beethoven, more Beyoncé. If anything, a choister is far more social as a single gal than she is when in a relationship. Indeed, many twentysomethings these days actually end up choosing to be single because there simply is so much going on. Meaning they have such a rich social life that adding on a mediocre boy toy seems like one too many weekly Krav Maga classes. Listen to Jennifer M., twenty-nine, who says, "I've definitely spent the majority of my adult life single, so the times when I do have a guy around, I feel this instant guilt, like I am not spending enough time with my friends."

But your friends will always get it because choisters are fiercely loyal, in a *Godfather*-meets-lip-gloss kind of way. Girls from the suburbs suddenly start channeling bad stereotypes of New York. "You shut your mouth 'bout my Susan!" We're like gangs, but without the guns or tattoos or even any rival gangs. We tend to walk around together, though, and to snap our fingers whenever *West Side Story* music comes on.

Weirdly, at the heart of our interest in being single is often our desire for connection. Just think of the many Lifetime Movies of the Week where the girl with the boyfriend—*and only the boyfriend*—feels more alone than the single girl with the great friends. From these highly realistic dramas, we learned that it is usually this girl with the boyfriend—and only the boyfriend—who will be found killing someone, sleeping with her baby-sitting charge, or getting hospitalized for an eating disorder. We're not saying that will *definitely* happen, but play it safe and keep in touch with your friends. A study published in the sociology journal *Contexts* shows that married people are less involved in the lives of their friends and family than are singles. A *San Francisco Chronicle* article summarizing the findings says, "Adults who have always been single are more likely to visit, contact, advise, and support their parents and siblings than are the currently or previously married. Singles are also more likely to socialize with, encourage, and help their friends and neighbors."[8] We love that since this totally common sense information is given robotically, it makes it scientific. Your friends are very familiar with what happens when you move from single to coupled—and when they do get you on the phone, they'll tell you all about it in slightly less polite terms than you've been "less likely to socialize with, encourage, or help" them.

Knowing what we do about the crazier side of the single scene (steaaady—more on that in a bit), it's much easier to find a make-out partner than it is to find a friend who will watch *Beaches* with you again. This means that being single in 2010 is not about being old Nell in the woods speaking to tree frogs. Rather, today's single means never having to say "I feel lonely" without someone to listen to you and give you brownie batter off the spoon.

But there is a self-perpetuating cycle at play—the more friends you have that are single, the more you want to join the party. Because it is a party. The nights of sweaty booty shaking and tequila do eventually distill down to support and connection, but they're mostly just fun. We've seen millions of images and movies of girls drinking, talking, and giggling together as if they're auditioning for a tampon commercial. But for once, Hollywood's gotten it right because those moments really are as fun as they look. They're so fun, in fact, that when played out against the backdrop of sexy bars, cute shops, and activity-filled cities, it's hard for the single girl to remember ever not living this way.

Many choisters cite female friends as their strongest social bond. Erin K. says, "I love men. Really, I do. Men, with their charm and inherent 'I don't give a fuck' attitude. But women create a sense of community and support for me. A year has gone by since I have seen most of my girls, and I didn't quite remember what was missing. I miss my girlfriends; I miss them for so many things . . . for all of their collective strength."[9]

For our generation, the incentive to spend time with friends is high, and female friendships provide much-needed therapy and feedback. Of the many genius points in this book, this is probably 2 or 3 on the scale of groundbreaking. Women have always relied on other women to give them the support they need, but for us choisters, our friends have publicly and uniformly made a leap to family. In what seemed to be part marketing strategy/part social commentary, Carrie Bradshaw and the other *SATC* girls lived almost entirely void of relatives of any kind for a good six seasons plus feature films. In sickness and in health, they broke bread with each other. When Carrie finally did get married, it was her friends who showed up to cheer her on. Nary a parent or sibling in sight. Bad screenwriting or social commentary? You decide.

Ethan Watters's *Urban Tribes: Are Friends the New Family?* posits that twenty- and thirtysomethings have foregone marriage and kids in favor of a different kind of family—one composed of friends. As Watters explained to his own friends when asked why he hadn't married yet (he got married later, actually): "I've been thinking that, for me, the problem is you guys . . . I mean, how would I get up the momentum to get married when I'm always hanging around you guys?"[10] Sometimes this family of friends enables choisters to put off starting new relationships that could tip the dominoes toward marriage. But it also keeps us content enough to prevent us from marrying the first guy who shares our love of laaaazzzyyy Sunday mornings. Because it takes more than that to compete with the people who know you best in the world—who know not to interrupt you during the Oscars, who know to give you room when the wrong presidential candidate wins, and who interfere when you start being weird about food.

For the choister girl, college was girlfriend-relationship boot camp, and we are desperate to maintain that intense intimacy for as long as possible. When Amalia decided to move to San Francisco with four college friends after graduation, they quickly realized a five-bedroom apartment was too ambitious, so they agreed to look for two apartments within walking distance. The Craigslist gods are benevolent and nondenominational, because Amalia and her friends managed to find two apartments in buildings twenty feet apart from each other. This meant that they were able to scoot down the prostitute-ridden street in their pajamas with a bowl of popcorn just in time for "After the Final Rose."

Stacy S. R., twenty-five, explores this idea in more classy terms: "I love my boyfriend, but I don't want to live with him. I'm very conscious of my boundaries: 'I want to live NOT with you. I want to live with my friends.'" Her friend Virginia H., also twenty-five, tells us, "Living with friends in particular is probably another way we can put off settling because you don't feel lonely." Meg R. pipes in: "That's why my therapist tells me to stop spending time with my girlfriends." The takeaway of this friend-as-family phenomenon again points back to our conclusion that being single does not mean being alone. The intense emotional connections we forge within a nonromantic framework undermine the historic monopoly on "happiness" held by relationships. Not that a friendship can give you everything a relationship can, but when you think of the long-term companionship alleged "adult" relationships are meant to provide, friendships are actually nipping at relationships' heels.

We'd even argue this friendship boom has long-term benefits. Yes, even past the point when we all buckle and get married. Virginia H. tells this story: "My parents just had their thirtieth anniversary, and to celebrate it they invited their fifteen closest friends to an elegant dinner. And the toast that my dad gave—it wasn't for my mom—it was for their friends, and he said, 'Without you guys in our lives, this never would have worked.'" Single tear. Oh wait, it gets nicer. "My dad continued—'You guys are necessary to be our best version of ourselves for each other.'" So remember that next time your boyfriend asks why your girlfriends deserve to spend the month on your couch. "Honey, she makes me want to be a better woman ... for you." Works like a charm.

Scientists agree: In a ten-year study of people aged seventy and older, scientists at the Centre for Ageing Studies at Flinders University in Adelaide, Australia, found that a group of good friends is more likely than close family relationships to increase longevity in older people. The scientists concluded that "those with the strongest network of friends and acquaintances were statistically more likely to be alive at the end of the study than those with the fewest."[11]

Hooray! Friends equal life! Put that in your bong and smoke it! And be sure to smoke it with your friends so that they can offset the health risks.

MEN STILL EXIST—AND WE LOVE THAT ABOUT THEM

Don't get us wrong—being single does not mean swearing off romance, or not having to wax your bikini line. See, when single, you get to go to dinner and bed with five guys every year instead of one.

"Dating" is what one historically does in the space between celibacy and a relationship, but choisters are nothing if not unhistorical. We know that a template date usually involves some food, some cologne, and some small talk about which movies make you chuckle, but it all sounds rather quaint and honestly a bit ironic— especially when it comes to his tongue in her cheek at the end of the evening. Quite frankly, such old-school efforts have become unexpected, undemanded, and while often admired, they can even be unappreciated. So we've found ways to bypass that chapter, and we often shudder at the formality of meeting someone at a designated time and place for what everyone knows will be an awkward experience. Some of us definitely do the whole doorbell-flowers-he-pays trajectory, and there is a growing movement to demand it as we get older. But let's just say that for the bulk of most people's single life, that's not how it's going down. It is just so much easier to run into an acquaintance at a party and accidentally sleep with that person and then start spending every minute together. Voilà! Relationship!

In theory, we should have learned to properly date in high school and college, but somehow that was one box that never got checked. As teenagers, most people couldn't take themselves seriously enough to try out the let-me-borrow-my-dad's-car-and-then-awkwardly-lean-over-the-gearshift-to-grab-some-sweater approach. So, they explored other options. They either became über-friends with someone of the opposite sex, and then after months of denial and 24/7 contact, they magically! shockingly! realized they "like liked" each other; or they did the normal thing—got drunk and fell on someone's face in a basement or at a concert. This then spread to college (more drinking, more face plants, varied venues), and soon you had a pattern of behavior that didn't stop with the cap and gown.

The point is, we've built all sorts of underground shortcuts to relationships and feel utterly unfamiliar with this "formal dating" territory. In 2008, Joel Walkowski wrote a great article for *The New York Times* titled "Let's Not Get to Know Each Other Better." In it, he recounts his own brush with the puzzle that is courtship: "A few months ago I liked a girl—a fairly common occurrence. But being slightly ambitious and drunk, I decided to ask her out on a date. This was a weird choice, as I'm not sure I know anyone who has ever had a real date. Most elect to hang out, hook up, or Skype long-distance relations. The idea of a date (asking in advance, spending rent money on dinner and dealing with the initial awkwardness) is far too concrete and unnecessary." He adds, "Riding my bike home, I realized I didn't even know what a real date was, beyond some vague Hollywood notion."[12]

Of course, the one regular exception to this problem is online dating, which eventually requires—for better or worse—a prearranged meeting in person. Americans spent over 500 million dollars on online dating and personals in 2005, according to a study conducted by Online Publishers Associate and comScore Networks. This constituted "the largest segment of paid content on the web other than pornography."[13] We would really love to see a Venn diagram of how those two populations intersect.

In 2002, Rufus Griscom, the founder of Nerve.com and the chair of Spring Street Networks, which powers personals sections for *Jane* and *Salon,* predicted that "twenty years from now, the idea that someone looking for love won't look for it online will be silly, akin to skipping the card catalog to instead wander the stacks because 'the right books are found only by accident.'" He continues, "We have a collective investment in the idea that love is a chance event, and often it is. But serendipity is the hallmark of inefficient markets, and the marketplace of love, like it or not, is becoming more efficient."[14]

Most importantly, online dating isn't (just) for dweebs anymore. From JDate and eHarmony to Adam4Adam and Love From

India, you've really got everyone covered. Claire, with the most online dating experience of our trio, gets a little too animated about it all. As is her way, she took it to extremes as a single gal, doing it in strange countries and other languages and using it as a platform to network about, well, *anything*. These days, she just uses her powers to convince others; within our circle of friends of friends, we know of three Match.com weddings last year alone. Although Claire didn't meet her boyfriend online, she was set up with him by the founder of an online dating site—so it all counts, right?

Of course, online dating sites aren't the only places people meet each other. But with the usual sources—work, friends of friends, friends of people throwing parties, people standing next to friends in bars—you have to be more careful for fear of slowing other wheels you've set in motion. Lucy M., twenty-five, had just started a new job at a television network in Los Angeles when a lovely young man at the next desk over caught her eye. Lucy was single and ready for a relationship, but decided against pursuing this romantic possibility because it might negatively affect her job performance or enjoyment. Just one more example of the bizarro game we're playing in which jobs trump boys and people first meet via avatar.

LET'S GET PHYSICAL, PHYSICAL . . .

But avatars don't *do it;* you need real people for that. So here we are. It's time to talk about the sex that happens outside a relationship. We find ourselves at the intersection of Vague Flirtation Road and Filthy Sex Lane—otherwise known as The Hookup. Ah, the term to end all terms. Who hasn't engaged in the ever-embarrassing act of having to explain to some older person or foreigner what they mean when they say "hooked up"? For a phrase that's as common as water in our daily vernacular, there's an awful lot of ambiguity surrounding it.

From a language perspective, it's genius. It's vague enough to seem illicit, it's entirely nondescriptive, and it is used casually and frequently enough that it would be physically impossible for it to always mean sex, right? Right? Lara's poor parents keep asking for an explanation, hoping that after hearing it spill from their daughter's mouth into daily phone calls it will someday start meaning "met for intellectual book group."

Hooking up has been noted all over the media: It's quite the phenomenon. And it is hysterical to those of us actually doing it to read up on the studies, quantifications, and qualifications surrounding this term. At the Institute for American Values (can you see where this is going?), they attempt to wrap their minds around our behavior: "On most campuses today there is a widely recognized practice, usually called 'hooking up,' that explicitly allows sexual interaction without commitment or even affection."[15] A bit bleak, but yeah . . . basically. We are not going to try to create some definition for the phrase—it can be sex, it can be less, it can be more (more?). It can be under the shirt, over the bra, in the dark, or just about in and out of anything. You can hook up with a person just once or enjoy repeated sessions over a period of weeks, months, or years. It's really up to you. It's an inspired, amorphous term meant to titillate, obscure, and reveal everything while saying nothing. In other words: It's a linguistic Dita von Teese. According to Kathleen Bogle, a professor at La Salle University, hooking up has spread like an epidemic because, as she's quoted in *The New York Times,* of "the collapse of advanced planning, lopsided gender ratios on campus, delaying marriage, relaxing values and sheer momentum."[16] Momentum toward penises?

So there you have it. And to those critics who say "You're not in college anymore, so pick up a phone and ask someone out," we say it's hard to fix what ain't broke. Because the hookup can be a beautiful and wonderful thing, especially in a social scene that in the postcollege decade still seems remarkably similar to our college years. Surrounded by choisters, the magic of the hookup is that you get to ride it right out of college and into tiny apartments and urban chic wine bars everywhere.

Surprisingly, *hooking up* is used to cover the worst of sins much less often than you'd expect. In fact, according to the Centers for Disease Control and Prevention, we are sleeping around less than others in recent history.[17] And the hookup does not connote bad, anonymous, scary sex. It's usually someone a couple degrees away from you whose company you probably enjoy (or have for the past few hours). It can be a harmless event in which a person likes another person and they agree to spend some time touching. Each other, that is. And probably on a soft surface.

So what do we get from these interludes? It's the quick fix—you don't have time for a boyfriend, but a girl's gotta eat. And from a psychological perspective, it feels better to have three guys instead of one (not necessarily at the same time) say, "Mmm, you're hot." A friend of ours once said that she no longer felt validated every time her boyfriend put a move on her because it was a battle won long, long ago and, as she said, "Of course he wants me. He's my boyfriend." At a certain point, we agree. The boyfriend's wandering hand is a little bit like your mother saying you're beautiful. It's not objective, you've heard it a thousand times, and it can't compare to when the makeup artist at MAC says the same thing. Somehow a new guy copping a feel is fascinating feedback—really? I'm hot?! Tell me more. . . . Whereas your boyfriend reaching for your ass is old news because you know his needs and you also know when they were last met. In that so many of us never tire of hearing that we're desirable, there's something about conquering new conquests that lets you feel like you're collecting important data.

Of course, STDs—and especially HIV/AIDS—make this more serious than we're suggesting, especially if you're not using your head and/or protection. But thanks to the not-so-recent sexual revolution, sex education, and the power of the constant public conversation about sex, society gave us the go-ahead to "explore one's options" from an early age. The combination of women's economic freedom, distance from home, and the advances in birth control discussed in the last chapter has created a wonderful mix. In fact, according to our survey, 37.5 percent of choisters said they expect to have more than ten sexual partners before they marry. And while not everyone assigns a number to their single years, most hope for a plethora of sexual experiences before they end up with any lifelong partner . . . if they expect such an ending in the first place.

Premarriage checklists used to include things like high school degree, ability to make pot roast, and light petting (*such* a gross term). Nowadays, the suggested skill set has not only expanded but diversified, too. The list of modern single expectations includes new rites of sexual passage: foreigner with accent, same-sex dabbling, regrettable night followed by walk of shame, first love, passionate love with wrong partner, one-night-stand-turned-relationship, older man/younger woman, lead guitarist.

To be clear, this is not just us. Simone G. tells us, "He was absolutely not a potential boyfriend, but when that college-athlete-turned-model is entertainingish, you go. And there were others—guitar-playing emo type, rich and entitled prick, etc. I have never regretted the number of guys I've been with, or my tendency toward the wrong boys. And now that I'm settled, I'm happy to have had some fun to reminisce about. It hasn't messed with my good relationships any, and by year twenty of marriage, I know I'll be only more happy I did it." It. Them. Whatever.

When asked for her tales of sexual dalliance, Delilah R., twenty-nine, said: "What do you want to know? That I enjoy being submissive with Greg, or how I tried dating a girl last year or being a swinger with Sam because I felt like I couldn't function in a normal relationship, or how I broke up with Eric, who I thought was 'perfect,' because I found out a month in that he had the smallest penis I've ever seen?" She kept going, but we stopped recording so we could focus.

Rachel Kramer Bussel, erotic writer and *Best Sex Writing* series editor, says "I think my generation and the one before it and especially the one after me are much more open to things like threesomes or what might have been called 'experimental' sex, whether it's BDSM (bondage and discipline, sadism and masochism) or public sex. Sex isn't quite as laden; that's not to say it's cold, unemotional sex at all, because it's not, but we don't think there's anything wrong with having a one-night stand if that's what we're into." As to why this shift has occurred, Bussel ventures, "I do think women are more interested in not settling down immediately and being more open to experimentation. I don't think all of it's brand-new, because there was a sexual revolution in the '60s and '70s, but I do think women feel less guilt and less like there's one right way to be sexual. I think my generation isn't as wedded to monogamy; we can understand the nuances of sexuality. We're less likely to think men looking at porn is cheating and more likely to want to find our own porn."[18]

While we're all for sexual exploration, we don't want you going away from this thinking that we're dismissing the high risks involved with this behavior. There are negative consequences to all this fooling around that go far beyond the diseases and pregnancy we've touched on. For starters, there's the sadness of a failed hookup: One friend tells us, "I was hooking up with a friend, which made things very emotionally awkward. Suffice it to say that the phrases 'dry as a desert' and 'I can't feel anything at all' factored into that failed encounter."

But more seriously, when playing fast and loose, you're bound to have at least one disastrous night that can leave you, at best, emotionally screwed. Sometimes it's because you want more than one night, and you end up waiting around for them to call. Rejection simply sucks, and it's often the searing feeling that many of us recall when we look back on our past romantic disappointments. And the worries of seeming too easy and too fast come from both personal and public venues—*slut* is still a well-established social insult that no girl covets in name or in feeling. Pushing your sexual boundaries, therefore, can fuck with your personal sense of value—and that's not something we advise messing with.

The same sexual freedom that's allowing all this fun is also establishing new definitions of boundaries right and left. The "being accidentally kissed by a member of the same sex" doozy has done the cocktail party rounds, and most of us know more than one dimpled sorority girl who has unknowingly walked into (and maybe/maybe not run from) an awkward threesome or similarly "forward thinking" sexual moment she hadn't prepared for. When everyone's okay afterward, these make for brunch-time tales considered hysterical either for the thrill of discovery or the close call, but these are difficult situations for a lot of people. It doesn't take a viewing of *YPF* (*Young People Fucking*) to convince a choister that sex is complicated and that having just one partner forever (forevaeva) might just be a whole lot easier on your psyche and your physical well-being.

Every choister knows all this, but we're still out there hedging our bets, and most are winning by a landslide. Perhaps some of the new hunger for varied sexual experience comes from the fact that we talk about it so damn much. Ignorance is sexual bliss. When your best friend tells you that she met a guy who did the strangest and most brilliant things with his tongue, you begin a hunt of your own. The same thing also allows us to be envious when our friend gets honeymoon face as she starts dating a new guy, even if we're perfectly content in our relationship. Our "must-do" list expands with every swapped story, and in this age of close friendships, you're more likely to hear exactly what your friends are up to and less likely to judge them—allowing more tolerant norms to be established. Plus, what generation before ours could tune into other people's stupid sex problems every night at eight o'clock thanks to any number of reality TV hits? Surely we aren't the only ones who watched everyone's favorite New Jersey housewife mix up the order of things when she went on a first date with the suitor *after* the phone sex? Although the "currently sleeping with" status is not yet mainstream on Facebook, we're confident that it's right around the corner.

We hook up to see if we should date—we don't date to see if we should hook up. This opens us up to a lot of fun (and some risk), but maybe it's good that dating has become the holy grail. People should take it seriously! And we do. When we do it. If we do it.

OUT OF THE FRYING PAN, INTO THE FIRE

But turning to Alanis Morissette for a minute, we remember that you live—you learn. Choisters believe that you're more likely to choose something that really works for you (reliable guy, productive position) if you first explore some of your choices (bendy beach sex with cabana boy). Shitty and romantic moments alike, are critical to your eventual growth into a responsible, committed human, and don't let anyone tell you otherwise. The hooking up, the dating, the sleeping over—it's more than just adding notches to your belt because you can. Women, it turns out, have been stocking up on exploits for a range of healthy, logical, and *responsible* reasons.

In the grand tradition of choisters, it's impossible for us to commit to someone or something until we know *for sure* it's what we want. We've got to do our research. But how do you research men? How do you try out different types of people? So glad you asked. Because that's the fun part for most choisters. Today, a choister gal can sleep with the bartender, get to know the artist, try out the model, and let the broker buy her dinner. We test them out, we see what happens, and no matter what, we always walk away wiser.

Best-selling twentysomething author Karyn Bosnak explored this concept in her novel, *20 Times a Lady*. Delilah, the protagonist, comes to a point in her life where she wants to face up to her past experiences—all twenty of them. Why? So she can learn things, get it together, and maybe, just maybe, meet The One. The book is a novel but reads like nonfiction, say some of our own friends as they pore through diaries to match names to Facebook profiles and see where all those past loves ended up. Choisters have made an art out of repurposing past failed relationships and horrific one-night encounters—they're not just vague tales of heartbreak or embarrassment any longer; they're part of your growth.

Emma U., twenty-five, tells us, "I think the best way to find Mr. Right is to date Mr. Wrong." Well then lucky for Lucy M., twenty-five, who has dated the entire catalog of duds. "I've dated a guy who was a producer's agent but stole expensive spices from Ralphs for kicks, a guy who was addicted to porn, an anti-Semite of all people," she says, adding that she's Jewish. "You wouldn't guess it," she continues, "but I think all of these experiences have helped me become a better judge of character." One of our favorite learn-about-you-to-learn-about-me stories has to be from a dear college friend . . .

"It was our third date, so very much still in the 'You should be trying to impress the girl' stage, and we were eating at a Chinese restaurant. I said, 'Should we get an appetizer?' and his response was, 'Well, I think we have enough food.' Now, to some people that might not have been a big deal at all, but for me, not only did it show a level of not really caring about making me feel good, doing things because he knows that's what the girl really wants, etc., but it also showed something totally innate about his personality that made him a complete no-go. I like to indulge, particularly when it comes to food. So, having someone whose thought process was 'It's not rational to get an appetizer because we have enough food' was a personality incompatibility that I just couldn't handle. Needless to say, I ended things with him shortly thereafter."

Shana certainly learned. Hopefully so did he.

When we ask about her history with men, Jennifer M. tells us that the term "wrong guys" just sounds so negative. "I'm a hopeful person. For the longest time, I was like wow—I choose such free spirits, wow—they're moving to Hawaii tomorrow. And then I realized, actually, I'm quite a free spirit. And I wasn't really tapped into that. You learn something every time."

Delilah R. feels that dating in her twenties has definitely shown her both what she does and does not want in a partner. "When I was dating Drew, we shared everything together, loved the same things, confided in each other. But I felt like I was the dominant one in the relationship, and I lost respect for him over time. The next man I dated, Demitri, was the exact opposite. He was the definition of an alpha male, dominant, masculine. But, we didn't share the same interests, and there was an age gap of fourteen years. I have always thought if I could combine Drew—with his artistic sensibilities—and Demitri—with his success and sexual appetite—I would have the perfect man!" And he would be called Drewitri.

Examples from Hollywood abound, but we share a particular predilection for *Runaway Bride,* so we'll just go there. By the fourth time Julia Roberts's character Maggie tries—and fails—to walk down the aisle, she has almost married one of many different types of men and has explored her hippie/athlete/banker leanings in depth. However, as demonstrated in the movie via an extended "How do you like your eggs" metaphor, dating such different men is merely a symptom of her lack of self-definition. Not until she finally decides she is ready to know herself thoroughly does she meet and marry a man she is meant to be with.

Same concept, different fictional friend of ours: Carrie from *Sex and the City* once deeply typed, "Later that day I got to thinking about relationships. There are those that open you up to something new and exotic, those that are old and familiar, those that bring up lots of questions, those that bring you somewhere unexpected, those that bring you far from where you started, and those that bring you back. But the most exciting, challenging, and significant relationship of all is the one you have with yourself. And if you can find someone to love the you *you* love, well, that's just fabulous." It is. Fabulous AND trite.

Stacy S. R. recounts her sister's marriage at the age of thirty. "She'd probably had eight hundred relationships before she got to that point. I'm not even joking—she had more boyfriends than I've ever seen anyone else have in my entire life," she says. "And when my sister was twenty-nine, my mom started to get a little concerned and was like, 'Well, aren't you gonna stop breaking up with people?'" But when Stacy's sister got married, she was *sure*. "She had had a lot of experience—she wasn't twenty-three, wasn't like, 'Well, this is *probably* right.' She really vetted it out so maybe she will be happy in twenty years." Maria T.'s rather ahead-of-her-time grandmother warned that "men were like a buffet dinner and it was necessary to sample all the dishes before you knew which one was your favorite." Poor Grandma was actually upset when Maria got hitched sooner rather than later.

The obvious, Oprah-style truism at play? You have to know yourself before you can really bring the right person into your life.

Of course, the learning doesn't stop there. As in touch as you are with what-makes-you-*you*, you can't possibly imagine how much more you'll find out about yourself once you add sex, a need for selflessness, and someone else's quirks to the mix. Strange behavior, like watching your normally cool, collected self lose your shit over a suspicious text message, is a good sign to sit up and dig around your psyche a bit further. Clearly, dating takes some training. We're committed to successful partnerships (eventually), so all that dating and sleeping around is really just our process. We certainly enjoy the recreational perks of this stage, but we know enough to take serious margin notes.

Simone G., twenty-six, says, "When dating around in my twenties, I ended up falling for a lot of assholes, like everyone does, but they weren't all like that. A lot of them were just wrong for me. But it was amazing to date someone wrong for me and to find this whole sheaf of qualities that actually were important to me in that person. Turns out I don't need career goals as much as I need kindness and an ability to prioritize family. All that only happened when I stopped dating the guys I thought I wanted on paper and ended up falling for the guy I would never even consider. He and I didn't end up together, but he helped me pick better men, and he made me ready to settle happily into them." Meg R. expands on this theme: "It was practice, but I really always knew that we wouldn't end up together. I did respect him a lot and respected the ways that we were different and felt like it was good for me to not stay in my small world."

Angelica S., twenty-seven, sums it up for us succinctly and from the heart: "I have learned so much from dating in my twenties, it's insane."

In the end, dating around is a way to find out who you are and what you want, and you can't do that just by watching your single friends act like idiots—you've got to make a couple of whopping bad decisions (and a few good ones) yourself.

WAS IT GOOD FOR YOU?

So it turns out the single landscape ain't too shabby. Hell, this is the longest chapter in the book. But who wouldn't want to spend time with wonderful friends and hot hookups? And yes, we're aware that the hard experiences that accompany all this are out there too, but even those can make you a little savvier and inform your future choices. Getting to the right partner and the right state of mind eventually is a pretty impressive silver lining to the gray cloud of scurrying out of a man's apartment Sunday morning.

But what if these wonderful experiences don't lead to the expected culmination of marriage? Social psychologist Bella DePaulo, author of *Single with Attitude* and the "Living Single" blog for *Psychology Today,* assures us that being single actually looks better and better as you get older. We didn't see that coming either. Dr. DePaulo says, "In fact, it looks like single life is hardest at the youngest years of adulthood. That's when lots of other peers are preoccupied with hunting and fishing for partners, and you can really feel left out if you are single and everyone else seems to be paired up or in a quest to be. As you move into your thirties and forties and beyond, you become more sure of yourself, of who you are, what YOU want from your life, what is meaningful and rewarding to you."

DePaulo goes on to argue that many married couples "look to their partners to be their everything—their best friend, confidant, household planner, sex partner, vacation planner, coparent if there are kids, travel partner, and everything else. That can be fine for a while if the marriage is great, but it leaves such people very vulnerable. If the relationship sours or is ended by death, then you are left with no best friend, no confidant (not even someone to talk to about your loss), no travel partner, and so forth. When single people attend to a whole network of friends (and again, not all of them do), they don't have that same vulnerability."[19] You may not want Debbie Downer at your next party but the woman has a point.

Of course, plenty of single women wish they weren't, and lots of us have worked hard at times to not be. We are still programmed to see progress toward a relationship as a good thing, whether we know better for ourselves or not. So perhaps the greatest indication of the changing times is the attitudes of women *in* relationships toward the prospect of being single. What used to be the monster under the bed is now the temptation in the back of your head. It's no longer that women in a relationship are just sitting there in their ivory towers thinking, "There but for the grace of God, go I." They're watching their friends skip out the door, thinking, "I like tube tops. I like graduate school in Beirut, too. Where's everyone going tonight?"

We're hardly saying that women have no more need for men or relationships, or that being single is always a walk in the park. But how many of you have uttered the phrase "I think I just want to be on my own for a little while" and *meant* it? That's no small thing. That's being a choister.

DATING AND MATING

5

Men are everywhere. My problem isn't just picking one, but picking The One. To make this daunting task a little easier, I decided to write a list of all the qualities I want in a partner. I've designed a perfect composite of the best parts of every man I've ever known, dated, or seen on TV . . . a Frankenman. Since then I've been scouring Los Angeles for this honest, funny, tall, blue-eyed man who looks great in jeans and has an IQ of 130 or higher. Last week I turned down a second date by saying, "You're really nice . . . but I'm gonna hold out for Frankenman" and showing him my list. He pushed the half-eaten tiramisu aside, leaned across the table, and said, "You know you're going to die alone, right?" I smiled and said, "See? Frankenman would be more optimistic." And so my search continues.

—MARIE J., AGE 27

Lest we give the impression that all we choisters want to do is sleep with strangers and watch *The Daily Show* with girlfriends, it must be said that we like love. A lot. We chase romance, force D(efine) T(he) R(elationship) talks, and try to change things about ourselves so that our partners won't break up with us (No really, I *love* Frisbee golf).

Take, for example, our core group of friends. A few of them spent the year after college graduation backpacking overseas—how choister of them, right? Of course they spent half their time at Internet cafés checking to see if their various long-distance beaus had emailed recently and the other half drinking cheap wine to drown their sorrows when the guys hadn't. Having a deeply vested interest in the amazing opportunities around us doesn't mean we don't sometimes like to turn our backs on those options and instead spend ten hours curled up on the couch watching *Arrested Development* marathons with a steady boyfriend.

Our reluctance toward choosing, or in this case marriage, doesn't necessarily play out on a daily basis. You might be avoiding all conversations about where to live in twenty years, but that doesn't stop you from rubbing your boyfriend's shoulders when he gets home and creating "Our Story" collages. We—Amalia, Lara, and Claire—wrote a book about romantic indecision, but we challenge you to find better girlfriends than the three of us—even though at least one of our relationships is strained by long distance at any given time. One of us writes a daily good-morning note to her lover-boy, another will wake up at odd hours in her time zone to make sure he wakes up at the right time in his, and the last started a blog to document the things she misses on a daily basis about her boyfriend when he's away on business trips.

Clearly, being a choister isn't an either/or existence; in fact, one of our defining qualities is that we want it ALL. And for many choisters, that includes a familiar face to look at when we wake up. According to surveys we bullied people into taking, at any given time approximately 50–75 percent of us might be in serious relationships. Although we spent the last chapter detailing how the experience of being single has greatly improved over the last thirty years, choisters are still human. And don't all humans, in the words of Lyle Lovett in *The Opposite of Sex,* want a person who will look for them first in a crowded room?

Choisters *do* do romance; we just do it differently. We seem to have polarized our dating options, always either stopping short of a relationship or catapulting ourselves into something that looks an awful lot like marriage. For most of us, this trend began in college, when the most likely options for a Saturday night were to hook up with a nameless person made hot by sketchy basement lighting or to lie next to our steady on our extra-long twin beds, fingers interlocked, whispering about our noble future as political revolutionaries.

Dating in college was tough. There wasn't much gray area between making out and serious relationships; couples just had to pick one or the other. There seemed to always be a fork in the road, and you usually came upon it the awkward morning after a hookup. You either scuttled out the back door or stayed for the next three years. Who doesn't remember the Sunday morning migration of scantily clad ladies across campus, all returning from their conquests to sleep, journal, and giggle. Roxanne T. remembers the other couples, ones who "ate together, spent the night together, and went to the library together. They were attached at the hip."

Whatever happened to the days of dating Jim on Wednesday and Joe on Friday (you know, when everyone's clued in and okay with that happening)? Allison P.'s mother used to regale her with tales of dating multiple men at once in college. "Not in a slutty way," Allison is quick to assure, "but in the old-fashioned way, where it was normal to start seeing a bunch of different guys until you narrowed it down to one." So for people who like options, why have choisters divided the process of dating into something unusually casual or unusually committed?

FAKE IT TILL YOU MAKE IT

Perhaps most surprising for a group of people taking the long road to the altar is how many choister couples are *playing* married. It's like playing house except it's less about the plastic food and more about saying you have a headache on Friday nights. Choisters are able to approximate married life like no generation before, spending day and night with their sweethearts, intertwining their lives, and generally embracing premature domesticity. This might be seen as a promising step, proving we like intimacy, take love seriously, and even that we're working out the kinks (no divorce in 2020!) before we promise everything to one another. Or, it might be a clusterfuck in which we give away all our milk for free. Living together without the ring is kind of like how once you discover Forever 21 you'll never spend more than $12 on a shirt. (Claire says, "It's like once you discover PerezHilton you'll never read the news again," but we think she's not really understanding what we're talking about.)

Another twenty-eight-year-old says of living with her boyfriend: "The best part about moving in together was the absence of planning. Before that, we had spent every night together and, consequently, spent a frustrating amount of time coordinating schedules, packing overnight (or multi-night) bags, looking for parking, making emergency trips to his local CVS for tampons, etc. Once we started living together, all those frustrating hours and arguments magically vanished." Elizabeth adds that it also broke down any barrier she may have left up while dating. "I had trouble adjusting to stinky bathrooms (mine or his), actually letting him in on how many beauty products I use, and knowing he was seeing (or worse, touching) my dirty laundry."

Apparently, choisters prefer to speed things up before we slow them down. Before you ask why a generation hesitant about marriage insists on co-opting the institution's basest characteristics—monogamy, cohabitation, and the infliction of family events—you have to realize that we all prefer to try things before we buy them. Just like how you wish you could wear the dress to the event before removing the tag. (Maybe one of us has actually done this, and maybe her name rhymes with *Shamalia*.) If marriage means living with a person for some forty- to sixty-odd years, choisters figure they should sample the goods a bit. And while we certainly can appreciate the argument that it's nice to leave *something* for once you're married, we're too intent on controlling the outcome of our lives to care whether our marriage starts off with less of a bang.

We covered what it looks like to be single as a choister—so now let's check out the other side of that coin. If living together before marriage is a preview, consider this the 30-second TV spot:

- Caitlin T. and her boyfriend have created a joint "vacation" account into which they each put monthly payments for future jet-setting purposes. *Don't let the word "vacation" fool you. Bank accounts with dual access are serious stuff.*

- Celia T. has spent the last four Christmases with her boyfriend's parents and is on an automatic email list for all "funny" jokes and stupid cat pictures. *It's not just because you like them "as people," Celia. In-laws are never that much fun.*

- Cassie G., twenty-five, goes to the bathroom with the door open. It's like *Reality Bites*, but it's real. *Only someone who was really, sincerely playing house could stoop so low.*

If we seem to be highlighting only the less-savory elements, it's because we have an intimate relationship with them. When Amalia learned how to burp at the age of twenty-six, she defended her subsequent insistence on doing so by claiming that life was "too short to pretend you don't burp for the sake of your partner." Claire lets her boyfriends do her laundry, with little concern for the dirty articles they're bound to encounter. (We are entertained by the fact that Elizabeth from five paragraphs ago brought up this exact example as an *undesirable* portion.) And Lara has really let herself go. Well, that's not nice. But her days of halter wearing and glitter applying are long gone, and in their place are sweatpants and a T-shirt that boasts the logo of her NGO. And while some might view this romantic slacking as a sad turn of events, we know how nice it is to have a boyfriend who endures your numerous UTIs and *still* thinks you're sexy, pink pee and all.

WHAT'S IN IT FOR US? STABILITY

There's a routineness usually reserved for marriages that has now been claimed by folks merely dating. Nice coup, guys. But in truth, life isn't sexy. And we know that when you're six months pregnant and throwing up, you'll be glad your boyfriend has already chosen not to leave you all the other times you were ill, weepy, and angry at the world.

A true, biologically-driven, socially-subsidized perk of marriage is stability. It's nice knowing what (and who) you're doing on the weekend—a peace of mind once limited to those who had exchanged vows. But with the "dating" phase of relationships lasting longer and longer, there's no lack of continuity for unwed choisters. And as a smart friend once said, "You either work out the kinks of your relationship *before* you get married or *after*." Choisters vote wholeheartedly for "before."

Things you learn by dating Johnny for four years instead of four months before tattooing his name around your ring finger:

- ⊙ Johnny's passionate about his work, but Johnny's not very good at finding a job after he loses one.

- ⊙ Johnny treats you well, but Johnny doesn't like his mother very much, and he's actually kind of a dick to waitresses.

- ⊙ Johnny never stops finding you attractive, but you know that sexy thing Johnny's so good at!? Well it's his only trick. Hope you like it a LOT.

- ⊙ Johnny is really generous. Johnny also doesn't mind his ever-growing credit card debt.

⊙ Johnny loves to wine and dine you—but he also loves to wine and dine himself. On average, Johnny gains about five pounds. Per year.

These days, we're lucky to be able to test-drive Johnny first. Fifty years ago, when Johnny was being deployed or relocated for his job, he'd pop the question to Sally and they'd make the move as a married couple. These days, Johnny might propose they do the long-distance thing and that maybe Sally should join him in a year *if* she has a professional incentive of her own, and then they can cross other bridges when they get there. Couples are no longer marrying for convenience. In fact, they're enduring great *inconvenience* rather than getting married "prematurely."

There are things couples have to get done—like grad school and jobs in other cities—that they are not willing to compromise on. Such life changes used to be reasons to get married, but are now part of the mandatory obstacle course in the "Should I marry you?" decision process. Of the people we polled, most listed the same "necessary tests" of a relationship: traveling together, living together, family hardships, and personal life transitions such as school or job shifts—and most mentioned premarital counseling. Choisters are skeptical of marriage, and it shows when they date.

SHACKING UP

Living together is certainly the main perk of marriage we've appropriated en masse. According to the 2000 Census, there are currently about eleven million people in the United States living with a partner they're not married to.[1] Scandal! Indeed, U.S. studies show that 59 percent of young people believe it is alright for a couple to live together without intending to get married,[2] and 50 percent agree with the statement, "I consider a stable, long-term relationship just as good as marriage." Perhaps most surprising, 27 percent of Americans even believe that "the concept of marriage is not relevant today," as found in a 2006 Nielsen survey.[3]

Paul Glick and Graham Spanier wrote an article for the *Journal of Marriage and the Family* in which they argued that "there have been few developments relating to marriage and family life which have been as dramatic as the rapid increase in unmarried cohabitation," adding, "Rarely does social change occur with such rapidity."[4] We agreed personally, but then we also found numbers: Unmarried couples living together increased 72 percent between 1990 and 2000.[5]

So how do you know when you're playing marriage? It's pretty much a clue when you start arguing about who starved the orchid to death (Lara *did* tell him to water it). Or when one of you wants to chat while the other is checking his or her pores. Or when all your black bustiers have been shoved to the back of the drawer in favor of a thick, flannel grandma nightie.

And why do we want to live together? Well, for starters, it's not SUCH an alien practice. As Zheng Wu, sociologist at the University of Victoria, writes in *Cohabitation: An Alternative Form of Family Living*, "Cohabitation may originally have been the normative form of family living. For example, in England the distinction between marriage and cohabitation remained unclear until the passage of Lord Hardwicke's Act in 1754, which stipulated more stringent requirements for formal marriage."[6] Ah, yes—Lord Hardwicke. Of course, perhaps the reasons for cohabitation now and back then are different: wanting the PERFECT marriage versus social fallout from the Black Plague.

Although it might ring false to the ears of our elders, the truth is that many of us want to live with our boyfriends and/or girlfriends because we believe a trial period might allow us to judge the person and our relationship in its entirety, not leaving any nasty "surprises" for after the vows.

Ruby D. explains, "I suppose if I had it my way, it would be like baseball; I would trade the players every few years and sign new contracts. Some years I hit a home run, some years I don't, but at least I'm not stuck with Joe DiMaggio twenty years after his expiration date."[7]

For people who pride themselves on trying anything, this is a surprisingly risk-averse area of our psyches. Living together is a challenge that choisters undertake because they are addicted to testing their relationship as much as possible before deciding it's The One. Just like one of those annoying guys who wants to prove how strong he is and walks around telling people, "Hit me in the stomach! Do it! Harder!" we are willing to get the shit knocked out of our relationships if that's what it takes to know they're solid.

Certainly, there are many couples that decide to live apart until marriage. And then there's the segment that essentially live together but resist being categorized as such. To those couples we say: If you're at your boyfriend's apartment six nights a week, you're not living alone, you're living a lie. Though Amalia spent most nights sleeping on her boyfriend's extraordinarily uncomfortable bed, she refused to exchange it with the expensive mattress going unused at her own apartment because they *weren't living together*, and besides, she "works at home and likes napping." Good point, Amalia. In this case, your denial hurt no one but your scoliosis.

Some of us live together very intentionally. There can be YEARS of conversations (you think that's an exaggeration) about the meaning, the impact, the family reaction, the moves that might follow, the tests to pass before, and the hoops to jump through after. And some of us just slip into it. When Gertrude D.'s roommate moved out, her boyfriend started spending more and more time there. She says: "Slowly he just started being there for longer and longer periods of time. And before you knew it—BAM!—he'd given up his own place."

Gertrude, "BAMs!" are like "yada yadas"... there must be more to the story. You just didn't know the signs. So be on alert—and if you keep any of these items permanently at your boyfriend/girlfriend's place, it's only a matter of time: phone charger, an extra pair of glasses, tampons, workout clothes, Lean Cuisines, acne wash in the shower, and the preferred brands of toothpaste, loofahs, and candles that you asked him to buy.

It seems the gradual buildup of products—a sweatshirt, some contact solution—at your sweetheart's place is just the human form of pissing on your territory. And once again, it all comes down to putting the relationship through its paces. Do you still like me when my clothes take up an entire drawer? Yeah? Well, how about with my yeast infection medicine on your dining room table? HUH?! Choisters are idealists, and how can you claim perfect love if it hasn't been tested?

SEXCAPADES

So what, in the name of all that is preferable about having a bed to yourself, is the cause behind this ringless cohabitation? Why are we okay with *acting* married and not actually doing it?

Well, one BIG difference between our behavior between the sheets and that of our parents is that they had to hide it if they weren't married. We don't realize how lucky we have it, calling our parents to say hi while our boyfriends shower in the next room. Maria T. believes that the fact that spending the night together is socially acceptable actually increases the intimacy in many relationships. "My grandma always remembers that when she and my grandfather got married, she barely knew him, even though they dated all through high school and college." Maria continues, "So much of their relationship took place in public—going to dances and parties—that their time together individually was limited."

At Stanford University, as recently as the 1970s, women's and men's dorm rooms were separate. If you were visiting a friend of the opposite gender, you needed a pass to enter and had to be gone by lights out. It seems like a lot of hassle for some clumsy fumblings.

But most universities don't play by those rules anymore, and most of us are so far from home anyway that it's not even worth our parents' energy to try to control the way that we young people interact with each other. The large majority of students live away from home for college, and this alone means we get used to certain ways of life while not under their disapproving eye.[8] During college, many of us got into the habit of sleeping over at our boyfriend's dorm room, and postgraduation, this trend simply takes itself to the next level.

Also, when you don't have to sneak around, you're likely to squeeze in more sex. Less illicit, potentially less passion-filled, probably not as thrilling without the heaving chests and hidden rustlings . . . but we digress. With choisters traipsing off on romantic

vacations down the California coast only weeks after first mention-
ing the guy's name to our parents, it's hard to tell if these lusty
getaways are a symptom of changing times or part of the cause.
Under the guise of "travel," we visit exotic locations and (spoiler
alert) have premarital sex! We're not the first generation to use
a vacation as an excuse for tent-time activities, but since we are
the first generation to make travel a lifestyle staple, this practice is
becoming a habit. Choisters have learned wisely that if you stack
enough layers of activities in between you and the nasty then it dis-
tracts parents from the reality at hand. "Spending the year traveling with my boyfriend was the best," says Morgan C., twenty-eight.
"My parents were glad I had a man's protection—even though 'living together' was clearly taboo."

Because parents have gotten used to the idea of our sharing hotel rooms with boys, there's a bit less expectation for us
to stay pure and in our own apartments. Emily W. moved in with
her boyfriend when visiting him (for a few months) in Paris. She
wasn't planning to, but France is expensive and he had packed the
toothpaste. Needless to say, the only things missing were registry-
inspired kitchen gadgets and any explicit parental discussion of
who was going where at what times of night.

Money is a big incentive—and a great defense when explaining your position to wary parents. The whole "why pay two rents
instead of one?" logic holds considerable weight with even the
most traditional families, especially because many of us choisters
live in some of the most expensive cities in the world—your New
Yorks, Hong Kongs, San Franciscos. When you're already spending
most nights at your boyfriend's apartment—or he at yours—the
monthly rent check for a one-bedroom across town is hard to

justify. Although the thought of Sally F., twenty-four, cohabiting with her boyfriend made her parents a little uneasy, the thought of unnecessarily spending $12,000 a year violated a more important life policy—that of avoiding poverty. So even for wary parents, faux marriage may be bad, but destitution is worse. As Jamie R., twenty-seven, says, "My parents said something like 'Of course you'll live together—how else will you find out whether you're compatible! Or afford the rent!'"

One of the reasons we play married is because we can. After all, being a choister is just as much about taking advantage of all these newly available opportunities as it is about having a different perspective.

CLOSE AND YET SO FAR

For every choister couple that cohabitates, another is whispering sweet nothings to each other from five hundred miles apart. Launching two separate careers can leave you and your partner in different cities; as can one person's need for soul-searching and the other person's need to pay off student loans. We ourselves have been at least three thousand miles away from our boyfriends for regular periods in our current relationships. But how do you reconcile dual callings within a single relationship? With help from Gchat, emails, Skype, iChat, text messaging, BlackBerry voice notes, and adult games of Scrabulous (fifteen points for *cunnilingus*). Technology has not only changed the way we behave while single and interacting with fifty Facebook flirtations, it has also affected the way we interact with our special "one."

But every modern advance brings a new range of setbacks. There are the omnipresent technical glitches—"I can't see you. Can you see me? The video is cutting out. You're frozen. Please don't ever make that face again"—but we're talking about something more fundamental. Consider the young woman who's shocked—SHOCKED!—when her fellow can't muster the energy to be a fully committed boyfriend after months of texting "i lik u" from across the world. As you will find out when homeboy gets home, it can be good to demand more from a person or a relationship. And technology sometimes lets partners off the hook, making life and love easier than it should be. When you're three hundred miles apart, you can screen your calls when you're in a crappy mood. Good luck with that when the two of you are stuck inside a three-hundred-square-foot apartment.

For those at home or abroad today, there are a hundred new ways to communicate with your partner; which might mean that you're doing more of it, but also that our communications are somewhat compromised. After all, there's only so much to be conveyed in 140 characters. Indeed, the wonder of video Skype is that it can occasionally take the pressure off you to talk. You can just sort of sit there and make cute faces at each other.

Everyone says that long-distance relationships are hard. People worry about fidelity, commitment, and comfort. But as we've heard from our survey participants—and witnessed ourselves—there's a certain ease to them, too. What better "have your cake and eat it too" scenario than having a boyfriend AND all the time in the world to devote to your friends, career, and commitments outside of Him (no, not *Him* Him). The lonely nights without the partner just aren't that lonely most of the time—which means more and more choisters are willing to make that long-distance leap.

GREAT EXPECTATIONS

Dating someone at a distance doesn't mean dating down. With all the flannel nightgowns and frozen iChats, our relationships might appear slightly compromised; however, our end goals are anything but. Certainly our romantic fantasies are tempered with pragmatic theories. Our parents and grandparents were focused on the GETTING married part. We're obsessed with the STAYING married part. An important distinction.

Although a twenty-three-year-old who's thinking she's ready to get married will surely value different qualities than a twenty-eight-year-old, all choisters are idealists in love. No matter our age, choisters are intent on getting things right, so we evaluate our boyfriends based on a set of very rigid love metrics. Our checklists. God, our checklists! The problem we've created for ourselves is that the longer one waits to get married, the higher the expectations grow. 'Cause if it's not going to be whirlwind, then it better fucking be foolproof. So we want our partners to be extraordinary Renaissance people. Here's a list of qualities. Can you imagine a SINGLE one you would be okay *without?*

> - Smart (maybe even smarter than you, but just not aware of it . . .)
> - Handsome (but not too concerned with his looks, or yours for that matter)
> - Funny (but thinks you're HILARIOUS)
> - High earning potential (but only casually—no money obsession or pyramid scheming here!)

- Wants kids like you do (or doesn't like you don't)

- Good in bed (and amazed by your prowess—"howdidyoudothat?" has crossed his lips more than once)

- Lets you watch the crap TV you love (maybe even sits on the couch and doesn't make critical comments when you cry at the Biggest Loser finale)

- Gets along with your mother (almost as much as with his own)

- Is fine with you working OR not working if babies arrive (hey, he's easygoing like that, and phrases like *paternity leave* are part of his vocabulary)

- Social (but not in a way where you don't feel like the most important person in the room)

- Etc. Etc. Etc.

At first you'll email us saying we're looking for the impossible. Then you'll email us again saying you found such a man! And we'll respond saying we told you so.

It's not that our mothers would disagree so passionately with this list. They themselves would say they wanted a sense of humor or someone to make them feel attractive. But our checklists are detailed, increasingly seared into our brains with each failed relationship, and worst of all, expected. We hold up each fellow to the list to make sure he looks good from *all* angles. Whereas generations past might have said "I met George, and all my expectations went out the window!" we'd counter by explaining that our expectations have been tattooed on the smalls of our backs and aren't going out anything. Choisters will continue to search far beyond when past generations would have given up on Mr. Right and given in to Mr. Persistent. And so their list becomes longer . . . and the right men harder to find . . . and then parents' sneezes start sounding suspiciously like "Breed!"

WHERE THAT LEAVES US

There's not even a word for what we do. I mean, is it really appropriate to say that people who have been together seven years are "dating"? *Girlfriend* and *boyfriend* work as terms until the altar. And *partner* always sounds a bit enigmatic. So where's the good verb? Where's the "We're BLANK-ing" that most adroitly communicates the fact that you're somewhere between having your DTR talk and birthing your first child. Why do people who've been dating for a third of their lives have to be grouped in the same category as someone who can't remember the other person's birthday? It just ain't right. So let's come up with a word. You can participate. One of our boyfriends originally proposed that we be fuck-buddies. Except in an effort to be more charming he said "love-buddies." So let's toss that into the ring. Thud.

You know things have advanced to a serious stage when the only change a wedding would bring to your life is the stress of planning a party. At one point, Amalia—who had been poring through bridal magazines since she was two—realized that her attitude toward weddings had shifted. Her knee-jerk reaction no longer went, "I'm gonna be so PRETTYYYY!" Instead it was more of an "Ugh, that'll really crowd my to-do list." Suddenly we're having conversations with friends about what we'd rather do with the money (medical school debts, travel to Rwanda, buy nachos, etc.).

Because much of the old significance behind weddings (Yay, we can live together! Yay, you can make me breakfast!) has disappeared. Now it's more like, "What's the point again?"

So we engage in relationships differently, both because we have that option and because we think it will guarantee us a more secure "happily ever after." It's not that our long-term goal has changed; it's just that we think we need to do some more prep work if it's really going to be *long*-term.

You know how they say "live like there's no tomorrow"? Well, we love like there are an indefinite amount of tomorrows. Because the truth is, there are! There are 365 days in a year, which means that if you're married for fifty years, that's 18,250 mornings you're waking up to your spouse's face. So you better be SO FUCKING happy with that face. And this, ladies and gents, is among the many considerations that go into choister love.

Perhaps what's happening is that choisters are beginning to think a little more like the bowerbirds. (Just go with it.) In an effort to attract his ladybird friend, the male bowerbird has to build a highly decorated structure using a variety of objects he has collected (bits of shells, leaves, flowers, feathers, stones, and berries—"Ooh! An artist!" the female bowerbird probably thinks). At mating time, the female will go from bower to bower, inspecting each and watching as the male bowerbird conducts his elaborate mating ritual. It's clear that only half of this metaphor works—the female half. For all the bower hopping we do, it'd be nice to see men up the ante and buy a bathmat or something. But the point is that the bowerbirds take their time! From where we stand, you get what you put in.

So there it is—we've got options outside the marriage paradigm that allow us to make a hundred small decisions instead of the Big One. We believe that this expansion of relationship options is only a good thing—and in time, we'll have the lowered divorce statistics to prove it.

LITTLE WHITE CHOISTER CHAPEL

6

I do this thing where for two months I'll be like, my boyfriend and I are going to get married and he's the best guy ever, and then for two months I'll be like, eh, if he breaks up with me tomorrow I'll be okay. But then I'm like—well, what stage will I be in when he proposes? Like, shit, what if he hits the wrong month? Cause sometimes I can't keep my hands off him and sometimes I'm apathetic and feel like he's my brother.

—SONIA F., AGE 29

Lindsay S., twenty-six, refers to the make-or-break juncture we all hit in every relationship as a Blackjack Moment. You come to a place—whether it's two weeks or five years into a relationship— where you'll either decide you're happy with your partner despite his flaws (the choice to stay at 17), or you'll say "hit me!" leave behind the safety of a known quantity, and trot off in search of a 21, knowing full well that every subsequent hand may be even farther from the mark. (Let it be known that this metaphor took twenty minutes to construct, and Claire still doesn't know why we're not aiming for 100. Hire us to earn your gambling millions, people.)

A disclaimer before you start rolling your eyes—it's not that choisters are looking for a perfect person; it's that we're looking for a perfect-for-*us* person. For example, Lara wants a man who embraces her love of travel, but she doesn't care if he smokes a cigarette or two. Amalia is fine with a big ego, as long as the guy thinks she's the shit, too. Claire likes her fellows handsome, foreign, brilliant, multicultural-child-loving, and religious; so actually that's pretty greedy and we can all roll our eyes at her together.

We know gambling metaphors are overused at best, but the wonderful thing about blackjack is that it requires you to evaluate what you've got in your hand, guess about the unknown, and make a decision based on limited information. This is the heart of the choister dilemma. We can't help but feel like once we've decided to commit to someone or something that it might mean that we're missing out on the life equivalent of a 21. As a friend of ours once said, the only perfect relationship is the one you haven't had yet. Entering a committed relationship generally results in even the most secure among us wondering, at least once or twice, if we're settling.

Yup. We said it. THAT word. *Settling*. But, like everything, it's a bit different these days. Settling used to be what a forty-year-old unmarried woman did when she wanted kids and the only guy available was a dud; now it's what a twenty-eight-year-old thinks she's doing when she marries a guy who isn't quite as obsessed as she is with heartwarming TLC shows about the challenges of being a little person in America. Once again, the word *settle* has everything to do with expectations and the fact that ours are greater than any previous generation's. To "settle" once indicated a lack of choices; now it implies too many.

While choisters experience this fear of settling with many of life's big decisions, nowhere is it more exaggerated than in romance, as that is the arena of life where earth-shattering, soul-shaking experiences are allegedly possible (Shakespeare *and* Stephenie Meyer said so!). Hence all the scandal that erupted when Lori Gottlieb wrote an article titled "Marry Him!" in *The Atlantic* in March 2008. In a piece that must have been the most emailed item of 2008 next to that YouTube video of Christian the Lion, Gottlieb argued that instead of waiting for some unreal combination of chemistry, intrigue, and practicality in our mates, we twenty- and thirtysomething women should prioritize timelines and simply choose a "Mr. Good Enough."[1]

Gottlieb's own bio reads like a choister manual: She refused to settle for a subpar mate, found a career she loved, and managed to fit in the birth of a son by a sperm donor. Maybe not ideal, but pretty sweet. Except that then the woman who was holding out for Mr. Right decided that other women shouldn't follow her example. Crap.

Understandably, the article went viral among our girlfriends. "Traitor!" Claire wrote. And she wasn't alone—you couldn't see the words through the exclamation points that glutted our inboxes. After all, as true-to-form choisters, we're contractually bound to disagree with Gottlieb's conclusion. It is anathema to our way of life, because we believe there *is* a way to find a good partner as well as some core-quaking love! As Ruby D. says, "I'm no expert on love. I do, however, refuse to be in a relationship with someone I'm not in love with. That may make me too idealistic. It may make me too picky … but I refuse to believe that the only options are being alone or settling for something you know isn't quite right."[2] We're with Ruby.

But while we're not ready to embrace Gottlieb's advice, she did articulate an element of our predicament pretty damn well. In her article, Gottlieb ultimately equates *every* marriage with settling since none are a romantic ideal: "Marriage isn't a passion-fest; it's more like a partnership formed to run a very small, mundane, and often boring nonprofit business."[3] And in truth, choisters get this. We've seen the ins and outs of marriage within our parents' generation, and we realize it's not all about roses and wine and magic behind the bedroom door. On many levels, choisters are very okay with the idea that marriage is a practical choice.

Using language completely devoid of fate or cupid, Marie J. tells us, "I've recently started to believe that if I had really wanted to, if I'd been willing to commit, I could've made that relationship work and had a house, a husband, and the career of my dreams by now. Is it that simple? Can I just make a decision, make a goal, make a commitment, and make a future?" Marie boils marriage down to an issue of action vs. inaction rather than love. "If I played a game of MASH right now and my results were: 'House, Husband, two kids, Prius, Photographer,' could I just commit to my desire for these things and attain them one by one? Could I simply set out to achieve these goals, in spite of how my passion might waver throughout the course of my quest?"[4]

Gottlieb was right. And we choisters do tend to approach our marriage choices with a bit more cold, hard logic than was customarily employed in the past.

We even bring in seemingly disconnected topics like "science" to help us negotiate the peaks and valleys of love. Harper T. explains: "Being in a constant state of infatuation—or as our culture cutely calls it, 'being in love'—is chemically impossible for long periods of time," she says. "So therefore marrying someone because you 'simply can't live without' them is inadvisable. Compatibility, otherwise known as the chemical oxytocin, is what causes you to love someone, to feel peace and stability, to be content with one person for the rest of your life." Her judgment on the matter as whole? "Love isn't strictly emotional, and therefore marriage should be, at least somewhat, logical."[5]

Our concerns about settling have less to do with the choices in front of us and more to do with the act of choosing. As Meredith explains, "One or two excess thoughts of the opportunities you're missing out on are not likely to cause a rift in your life. However, if your whole life is full of tiny niggling thoughts of what *could* be going on versus what *is* going on, it can cripple you."[6] If the flip side of choosing one thing is foregoing everything else, then marriage necessitates the closing of many doors. Thus it's the loss of the unknown that somehow suggests settling, not the marrying of the known. For choisters, a lot of the chatter about marriage is not ultimately about the partner, but the *act* of picking. As if *settling* is a synonym for *choosing*. Allison P. tells us that for her, "it sounds so negative to 'settle,' but you can also think of it as shutting up the voice that tells you you can always find someone better." Choisters around the world in any stage of life would love to know—how do you get that voice to stop yammering on?

Look at the men your friends pick as evidence of our problem. We tend to really like our friends' partners (thank God)—but are they really the *best* ones out there for the best people you know?

As Emma U., twenty-five, says, "If a woman settles with a man, then other women think that she is going against the movement toward building a strong, independent life as a woman, or even achieving the fairytale by finding her number one—her soul mate." In a point that got us nodding, Emma continued, "Isn't it interesting that we call commitment 'settling down,' as if any kind of commitment is about some form of settling? I don't think that I would be one to settle, but I do think that I would be one to raise a child alone, to date many men because I don't want to settle, to pass up the one because I am too busy trying to make sure that I don't settle for the wrong one."

And Emma's right—"Would you settle?" becomes an important and defining question for every choister. Up there with "Is there a soul?" or "Do I sleep with people on the first date? What if they are very, very hot?" The reality is that some of us choose to hedge our bets, take no more cards, and walk away from the table down the aisle.

BUT YOU SAID . . .

Having just spent the last one hundred pages explaining to you why choisters are squeamish about marriage, we now need to make sense of the fact that each of us has attended five weddings this summer alone. How, you might ask, does the growing tide of nuptials not entirely undermine our brilliant choister theory that this world of choices has paralyzed us from making any real commitments? What happened to "love choices, hate choosing"? The answer is a good one. So good we're going to start a new paragraph with it.

This book is less about how the story ends and more about why the beginning looks so different. After all, we never said choisters don't marry. That would be daft! Think about it: 96 percent of people end up getting married, and we contend that a large chunk of people of marriageable age are choisters.[7] This means there are plenty of choisters tying the knot.

There is still a lot of glitter surrounding the Great Institution of Marriage, and we're not just talking about the "I Do" Bedazzled Hanky Pankys you're wearing under the dress. Most unmarried people (twenties to thirties people) fully intend and hope to be married sometime in the near future. Even Lucy M., twenty-five, a Los Angeles native who's entirely focused on her career and "can't be bothered with boys" admits to having "a shoe box of bridal magazine clippings that I've collected with my best friend over the years." So contradictory! But who can blame her? The engagement ring industry is booming, and the schmaltz of weddings is only growing despite the violently horrible economy. We grew up on *Father of the Bride,* we squealed when Chandler proposed to Monica, and we've all indulged in the occasional engagement porn that is the *Martha Stewart Weddings* issue.

There's no doubt about it: Choisters still want the happily ever after. And in a culture that still highly romanticizes marriage, we can't help but put most of our happily-ever-after eggs in the wedding basket. But while romance may explain how you end up with a beautiful bow when you tie the knot, it doesn't tell us why you choose to get married in the first place. Choisters see the world as a place that offers endless options, and if marriage takes most of those options off the table in the blink of an eye—what's with the obsession? In the nonstop buffet of casual sexual encounters, high-quality single time, and fulfilling unmarried relationships that is *la vida* choister, what would compel someone to suddenly order à la carte? Or, as we choisters are wont to interrogate our newly engaged friends, *You're doing what? Why don't you finish your MFA/MD/MBA/JD first? Are the rumors about fireworks and fat babies with arrows real?*

Or maybe they're all just preggers.

NOT YOUR PARENTS' ENGAGEMENT

There's a litany of reasons people choose to finally commit, but they usually have little to do with being in love. Yep, you read that right. As we've said, choisters *major* in love. But we can do so without getting married. We don't need a ring to pledge our hearts to one another. With so many loves in the choister life, and only one wedding (hopefully), we employ basic arithmetic to prove that love cannot be the only wedding prereq.

And what of the other *traditional* incentives to get married? As far as we can tell, these are twofold:

1. You believe you've found your soul mate,

and/or

2. you're scared you'll lose the guy.

But neither of these options is very typical for choisters because: 1) we've dated (and, yes, loved) too many people to believe, wholeheartedly, in the single soul mate theory, and 2) the idea that there are many great matches for each person lessens the threat of being left. If you can't have a soul mate, losing the next best thing is less brutal since you'll probably find another. As Amanda M., thirty-one, says of soul mates, "I hope there's no such thing 'cause it's kind of terrifying." Stacy S. R., twenty-five, calls the cosmic matching of soul mates' bluff: "Of the billions of people in the world, why would your soul mate have the locker next to you?"

Unlike previous generations, where couples got engaged quickly because they weren't *yet* having sex or living together, we're getting engaged as a final frontier. So if the motivators of yore are obsolete, what's replaced them?

HIGH CHASER

Like we said, engagement is a frontier, and we are nothing if not adventurers. Plus, we like our celebrations, and after our college acceptance letters have collected dust and friends have stopped toasting our lost virginity, we start to look around in search of the next triumph to write home about.

We've covered the choister relationship basics: You start dating someone; you sleep together (probably sooner than you meant to); you say "I love you;" you say it again, this time with feeling; you move in together. Then, after a few months, all the relationship highs are fading in the rearview mirror. The future seems to hold more of the same old, same old, no matter how funny/handsome/charming/perfect your partner might be. How to capture the adrenaline fuel of falling in love all over again? What else is that big a deal? Engagement.

In exploring engagement as an upper drug, let's turn to the addicts: the celebrities. Not many choisters are celebrities, but most celebrities are choisters. Britney Spears got engaged to Kevin Federline after dating for three months, Mariah Carey eloped with Nick Cannon after just a month, and Paris Hilton has pledged she'll "marry this one" about six different suitors in the last year. A regular choister in the twenty-first century has enough problems dealing with the range of options and decisions required to sort out a life. To that plight add unlimited money and extensive freedom, and you've got a choister to be reckoned with. If you are a celebrity, you can have anything you want. Free Starbucks (we're guessing), hotel upgrades, the leading man of your choice. So what do you want? How the hell do you know? Life is complicated enough, what with the antics of your new hairless, hypoallergenic mini poodle.

Result? Choister celebrity chooses everything, gets confused, messes up, falls hard, chooses more things, gets more confused, messes up more, falls hard, shaves head, ends up pantyless on PerezHilton berated by fans everywhere, only to be potentially restored through a Liberian adoption and/or UN peacekeeping mission with Angelina. But we digress. As celebrities attempt to use their social and economic power to take on *every* choice the world provides, they reveal to us the type of high-seeking and lifestyle alteration that is typical (in a *far* diluted way) among us choister peons outside of Tinseltown.

So what is one of the most common things that celebrity choisters engage in while screwing up? Love! In the world of romance, though, things get boring really fast. So you better have some new tricks up your sleeve—and breaking up and publicly making up ten times this side of Sunday ain't enough. If you're a celebrity—or even a plebian like us—how can you ensure the next romantic high? Play *the commitment ante.* In other words, up it. Enter engagement. Like Heidi and Spencer—twice! Or, even better, child before engagement. Or, child followed by ambiguous engagement followed by breakup followed by secret wedding, in close succession. Indeed, a disease that began among the beautiful people has spread down to the rest of us.

We have far fewer friends than most, and even *we've* seen two sub-six-month engagements in the past year. We know this issue is a favorite with the older choister set, who seem to happily skip away from eight-year relationships only to marry after eight months. Clearly, for all our talk about the value of tried-and-true certainty in a partner, even choisters can get swept up in a relationship's rip current.

Turns out that no matter the merit of the particular partnership, engagements are fun for all. And if you don't do it, you at least talk about it in the early stages of being mesmerized by your significant other. What a high! Talking about "forever" while curled up in bed is like the second cousin of walking on the edge of the Grand Canyon. A great thrill, provided no one gets hurt.

BACK HERE ON EARTH

There are, of course, more serious and respectable reasons to get married that don't have to do with some sort of love-junkie withdrawal.

For most choisters, the major impetus behind the wedding isn't the need to lock the other person down or to impress families on either side. Marriage is what you do before you have kids. It's the old wiffle-ball-and-chain. Yes, conceiving outside of marriage has become increasingly common. Hell, conceiving without a partner is nearly ho-hum. But the idea of actually maintaining a family unit outside of wedlock—holding your ground in that unmarried space—has not yet passed into the socially acceptable realm. We grew up in the comfort of a legally bound unit where people had the same last name and Mommy could visit Daddy in the hospital without showing an electric bill—and we want the same for our children. As Felicia P., a twenty-nine-year-old producer in San Francisco, points out, "You don't want to end up in a situation where your spouse is taking your kids and you have no rights to tell him that he can't leave the state."

Once choisters start thinking or practicing procreation, they head for the altar in droves. As Tara D., twenty-nine, says, "My boyfriend and I had been living together happily for four years without much thought of marriage. Who had the time to plan that kind of event? But once we both were touched by the baby craving, the reasons for getting married outweighed the ones against, and so we took the plunge."

Babies aside, getting married makes a whole lot of practical sense for a lot of couples, too. Try telling a medical school that you simply *have* to get into their program in New York because your boyfriend is located there. They will laugh at you. We know, because Lara tried—and now, Lara is going to med school in California. Throw in the word "husband," however, and suddenly you've got some pull. When it comes to life planning, job services, and student loans, having a husband rather than a boyfriend makes the world go round that much faster. And don't get us started on taxes (it's complicated and they're boring). The benefits of marriage in that respect have been proven repeatedly, if only as a right that is dangled cruelly over those who have been denied it.

And finally, there's the issue of outside expectations. While people do engage in all kinds of nontraditional coupling these days, marriage has been the norm for one heck of a long time, and that alone gives it a lot of social importance. Amalia told her grandmother two years ago to stop asking when the wedding would take place, but minding one's own business goes against every grandmotherly code. Recently Grammy told her, "Five Words: Don't. Let. Him. Get. Away." Amalia could have explained that her boyfriend hadn't even proposed yet and that his "getting away" was not an issue, but instead she thought: *Oh-god-I-really-should-just-get-married.* At a certain point, resistance takes more of an emotional toll than giving in. Meg R., a twenty-nine-year-old medical student in Northern California, sums it up: "It's just easier to say *husband* than *boyfriend* when you're forty." Or thirty, one could argue.

But don't think for a second that just because people choose to get engaged, they immediately lose their choister tendencies. Contrary to certain TV show suggestions from one-dimensional, usually male characters, marriage doesn't come with a lobotomy. So how can we have it both ways? Simple. *Choisterize* that shit.

IF MARRIAGE DOESN'T CHANGE CHOISTERS, CHOISTERS CHANGE MARRIAGE

In truth, choister marriages should be a whole other book—one we're not qualified to write yet but would gladly BS our way through for payment. But we've helped a few boys pick rings for our friends and have attended more than our fair share of nuptials, so we know what the tip of that iceberg looks like. After the proposal, there are a few ways to manage the engagement. A few styles, if you will, that represent your marriage attitude just as much as the cut of your jeans defines your degree of hippie- vs. hipsterness.

Engagement

When it comes to engagements, there are quieter affairs that wouldn't touch the Knot.com website with a ten-foot pole. The guests—all twelve of them—are invited through Evites and/or Google calendar, and people bring potluck. The proposal is more of a conversation, and the ring is something simple you'll switch from your right to your left hand once you're married (or the other way around, if you're going European). Tracy L., twenty-seven, knew the taffeta wedding wasn't for her, and her engagement reflected that. "My planning process consisted of planting some flowers that would be in bloom by the date of our wedding and calling our twenty guests by phone to make sure they could attend."

And then there's the *other* kind of engagement. Where fireworks are just one aspect of a multipronged approach to win the award for Best Party Eva. The rock on the ring? Mammoth! The proposal? Ready for its pictorial close-up on Facebook! The request of the father's permission? You bet your golf clubs!

That's right—for a generation raised by semi-hippies (give or take five years and a pair of bell-bottoms), a large percentage of choisters act surprisingly traditionalist when it comes to our nuptials. Claire wrote a paper in fifth grade on how the engagement ring came to be, explaining that it served as a symbol of the responsibility that a father passed on to a daughter's future husband. This was, of course, a responsibility that said daughter was in no way ready and able to assume on her own given her limited educational opportunities. You'd think Claire would eschew today's baubles as a result, but in fact, she has her eye on a one-karat, princess-cut beauty. Our mothers' fingers might be adorned with rockless bands or an aquamarine or two, but our generation is buying the big sparklers at alarming rates. A recent survey conducted by Brides.com discovered that the average cost of an engagement ring has climbed 43 percent since 2006 and now reaches a staggering $6,348.[8] And that's in mid-recession.

As explained by Meg R., "Not a single one of my parents' friends got a proposal accompanied by a big-ass diamond ring. But now my most intelligent, empowered female friends, who are on the same level with their boyfriends on every single thing—super respectful, super egalitarian—want the proposal, the ring, the whole nine yards." Roxanne A. says the same: "All my friends' engagements have been a big deal. From vacations to the Bahamas to proposing on the beach ... everyone I know has gotten a rock." After all, who is impervious to a multimillion-dollar industry intent on making you sparkle from top to bottom?

Typically, choister proposals are followed by speedily-planned trips to the Mighty Vera Wang and all the other white fluffy dress stores. Congratulatory cards once reserved for the wedding are now also mailed in response to the engagement, where they collect on fireplaces for all to see. When Lara expressed skepticism about the giving of an engagement present, she was in the minority. These days, you need to celebrate a wedding at the bachelorette, engagement, and bridal showers, *and* the ceremony.

Meanwhile, our hippie parents, who wed in their bare feet on a hill, look on with a mixture of delight and horror. Choister ladies typically invite an average of seven friends to be their bridesmaids. About this Amalia's mother once said, "You're not a queen, and you shouldn't look like you're holding court." We'll see how Amalia "Can't Hurt Feelings" McGibbon reconciles that with her ten best friends.

Engagements these days are like birthdays on uppers. Whereas people apologize if their birthday celebrations somehow stretch across more than one weekend, engaged parties feel entitled to at least a year of squealing cards and voicemails. According to a recent survey by the Condé Nast Bridal Infobank, the average American engagement has gone up from 11 months in 1990 to 16 months today.[9] Some engagements even last years. You know, the one that started with all the pomp and circumstance of champagne and presents but slowly just sort of *sat* there, not really doing much? We do. So does Pam Beesly.

Indeed, some choisters are brave enough to make the committed step to get engaged, only to freak out a few months before the big day and end up stalled in romantic limbo. It's kind of like not being able to make a decision about whether to go through the yellow light and then coming to a stop five feet into the crosswalk. After all, it's one thing to say yes to a man who's on bent knee and surrounded by roses and another to figure out which two hundred people you want to witness your "For better or for worse" pledging. All those concerns about choices and settling get louder in your head as you edit your spouse-to-be's sloppily-written vows, and like a schizophrenic with an up-to-date Haldol prescription, you realize how much quieter you are in this committed-but-not-cemented relationship.

THE DAY ITSELF

Once you make it past the engagement shindigs, there is still the actual day-OF to plan. There seem to be two different schools of thought: wedding as No Big Thing and wedding as The Ultimate Thing. In short, choisters either play down the event because they consider it a mere practical measure or turn it into a circus to proclaim just how "right" this choice really is.

The Nonwedding

The nonwedding is just what it sounds like. A trip to city hall, perhaps, or a Vegas elopement. A party of thirty in your back yard where the fanciest jewelry around is the dried noodle necklaces the guests wear to celebrate the summer solstice. The defining characteristic is the limited nature of the to-do. In other words, if you're throwing a nonwedding, you know who you are. Twenty-five-year-old Lucy M. says, "My wedding will not look like a Nancy Meyers movie, and I'm okay with that." Sonia F., thirty, tells us cryptically, "All I need is a beach and a pig roast."

Thirty-year-olds Sarah M. and Lucy D. went the understated route when they got married in San Francisco last year. "Our commitment to each other was clear by that point; the wedding was about making life's logistics run a bit smoother." And then there's eloping. For $119, you, too, can reduce the hassle.

If you'd like a nonwedding of your very own, try some of these tactics:

⊙ Pay for your wedding yourself. Y'know, with your independent woman-of-the-twenty-first-century status, instead of your parents' savings. Quick tip! Don't use the credit card, and you're bound to spend less.

- Keep the budget under $1,000. Tiki torches and citronella candles are key ingredients. A girl we know was too busy going into debt over business school to not be a wee bit budget-conscious at her wedding. So when she spotted the perfect wedding dress in a Fifth Avenue store, she bounded over to eBay and, $250 later, she was the most beautiful bride.

- Make your wedding a blip on the radar of your friends and family. Phrases like "It's really not that big of a deal" and "We're doing it on June 15—or maybe it's the 16" ensure this. If you're really quiet, no one will notice your relationship changed—including you.

- Write your own vows. Include mention of other partners, and say *polyandry* like it's not a dirty word.

- Make it a destination wedding. This might seem lavish, but it can be a nonwedding in disguise. If you choose a location that's remote enough, you'll be paying for far fewer chicken dinners.

The BIG Wedding

On the other hand, it seems that many choisters have decided that if they're going to wait, they are going to do it right-with-a-capital-R once it finally happens. After all, we're nothing if not perfectionists. In these scenarios, there will be white dresses, doves, and vintage wines nestled among the tables' tea roses. Apparently some of us feel the need to compensate for our revolutionary delay in marriage with über-traditional weddings.

In a way, having a big wedding is a bit like being the freelancer who changes out of her pajamas in the morning just to "get in the right mind-set." Fake it till you make it, if you will. No, we're not saying that big weddings are false, because invariably the two people are very much in love and will hopefully live happily ever after and then some. It's just that given all our hemming and hawing leading up to the main event, going extra BIG on our wedding day is a good way to psych ourselves up. One might argue that an $8,000 bridal gown and a fancy country club is the best pep talk you'll ever need to keep from being a runaway bride. It helps your guests too. A big wedding lets you finally sweep away the concern that's been building among your friends and family while you took your sweet time.

The mainstays of a big wedding are fairly obvious. Flowers, lobster, more flowers, people in outfits with trays passing out champagne flutes without carding you, something written in calligraphy, monogrammed iPod party favors, and twelve-piece bands. "I think weddings have gotten completely out of control," says Maria T., twenty-eight, "but then again, I have absolutely no ground to stand on as mine was over-the-top and extravagant." Beat. "And I enjoyed every minute of it immensely."

Not only are these parties expensive, but they are glorious opportunities to drag out and dust off all sorts of archaic traditions. Modern couples are suddenly acting, well, rather unmodern. Virginia H., twenty-five, confesses to being surprised by how many weddings she's attended in churches. "I'm like, 'What? I didn't know you were religious.'" And Layla S., also twenty-five, watched her older sister—a powerhouse lawyer who works eighty-hour weeks and kept her own name—plan the entire wedding with no help from her spouse. Because although the older sister and her husband *usually* pay no attention to gender roles, the nuptials were an exception. Naturally.

The same girls who, in college, either spent every day with their boyfriends or didn't date anyone are now choosing between the party of the year and the party that doesn't matter. You either have two hundred guests or twenty. Choisters tend to live in extremes, so committed are we to the path we decide to take. Or in this case, the aisle we decide to walk down.

The three of us aren't sure where we'll fall yet. Amalia loooves big sparkly engagement rings, but she's sure she'd lose it somewhere. And would it really match her stay-at-home-writer sweatpants wardrobe? Claire is partial to the idea of destination everything, and weddings are no exception, and Lara just doesn't think she wants a big to-do . . . but think of the gifts! And all of us are weighing the costs of one night against mounting postgraduate debt. But whatever we choose, whenever we choose, we're sure it'll be fun. Because all those years of single life have, at the very least, taught us how to feel truly, personally connected to all the Top 40 jams that every other bad white girl dancer is playing at her wedding.

we r ovr:
WHEN BAD THINGS
HAPPEN TO GOOD
CHOISTERS

7

What happens during a breakup that causes every single person you know to decide that they are the exact person to cheer you up with their incorrectly spelled, acronymed, numeric Facebook post?

"i hurd wut hppned. so srry. I <3 you. call u l8r."

—Bari S., age 21

So maybe you've been through enough iterations of the choister dating cycle to want to reincarnate yourself as a higher dating form. And maybe the specific pros of your partner outweigh the cons you associate with settling (Note to self: leave that part out of the marriage vows). In that case, you win the wedding, rings, and rice!

But maybe the price isn't right, and you'd rather spin the dating Wheel! Of! Fortune! one more time to see where it stops. Unfortunately, like with all good game shows, you have to qualify first, and this means ending it with your current partner. *Wanhwannnhhh.* Although this is hopefully just a painful means to a happy end, that happy ending can feel impossibly far away mid-breakup. Sadly, if you fit the demographic of this book, you are probably breaking up with someone, have broken up with someone, or are going to be broken up with by someone. Blech, hurl, gasp.

In discussing breakups, we'd like to reference that fine British film, *Imagine Me & You*. This 2005 romantic comedy is an excellent barometer of the trials and joys of choister life—if only because everyone in it is so overwhelmed. In brief (spoiler alert! we ruin the end to prove a point!), the trajectory of love in the movie is as follows: Rachel marries Heck. Love and roses rain down. They seem happy; then things change. Just-married Rachel falls in love with the female flower arranger at her wedding, while at the same time Heck decides to quit his soulless job and follow his dream of traveling the world. Rachel becomes wildly happy with the flower arranger, and Heck meets a hot woman on his flight. Implied happy endings all around.

So what's the takeaway? First, it's one of our favorite movies, and we wanted to talk about it somewhere. More important: It's not that choisters need to avoid committed plans like marriage to be their choister selves. But the movie *is* a reminder that in a world of options, choisters need to explore the paths that intrigue them so they can one day settle effectively. In the case of Rachel and Heck, acknowledging and exploring their true personal interests—even if it clashed with what was traditionally expected of them—may have helped them build stopgaps into their relationship, thereby preventing them from divorce in the face of wanderlust and lesbianism.

Rachel and Heck also showcase another important point: The list of reasons we break up nowadays is longer than it used to be. If you allow yourself to also list the *ways* you could break up with your boyfriend in these technological times, you start needing more space on your hard drive. One of those wonderful side effects of the age of options is that you really can get your heart broken any way you like. It's like Baskin-Robbins's thirty-one flavors, but less tasty and more excruciating.

BEFORE: THE WHYS OF CHOISTER BREAKUPS

The breakup phenomenon is anything but new, and choisters certainly have no monopoly on heartbreak. People have been cheating, lying, choosing someone else, acting selfishly, and falling out of love for as long as they have been dating. And on the flip side, people have been sobbing, feeling rejected, catching cheaters, and miserably asking "whywhywhy" for just as long. What an emotionally rich topic.

In the days that preceded the choister, relationships and their conclusions may have been a bit more concrete. Vague and unarguable reasons like "the timing is off" and "because it's too easy" were less common. In the past, Joe was an asshole, or Sally had cheated, or Joe needed to explore his free-love side and Sally didn't want that near her bed. Or perhaps Joe and Sally were dating other people and it just fizzled without too much love lost on either side. Seems when your timelines are shorter, you just might be a bit more practical about the breakup. By comparison, choister breakups seem anything but matter-of-fact.

When Simone G., now twenty-six, broke up with Scott, she said it was hard to explain to her mother why they had parted ways. "My mom kept asking, 'Did he do something wrong? Do you not love him anymore? Did he dump you? Did you cheat on him?' But it wasn't anything like that. I really loved Scott, and we were obviously compatible. I just really needed to be alone and to see what was out there."

Simone's mom didn't get it. Scott seemed nice, had a good job, supported Simone's goals, and they were in love. By this point, Mom's list of Things That Could Have Gone Wrong was exhausted. But she didn't ask about the tiny nagging feeling inside Simone that suggested there was more important stuff for her to do than Scott. Basically, Simone had a choister moment: Simone loved Scott, but since when was that enough?

Similarly, when Dan B. dumped Rene W., she was devastated. Particularly because there didn't seem to be any real reason for the breakup. Sure, he had talked vaguely about starting his own business and moving to another city, but she had always been supportive, saying things like "Of course you should follow your dream" and

"We'll work it out" in honeyed tones. But then he broke up with her, explaining that he "felt panicky about closing off options and having his life restricted in any way."

Relationships *can* feel restrictive, and no one likes that. In the memorable season three finale of *Grey's Anatomy*, the wedding for Sandra Oh's character is called off at the last moment. Her reaction to her fiancé walking out on her? To tear off her dress—to actually cut it off of her body—while crying, "I'm . . . I'm free. Damn it. Damn it, damn it! Oh God, get this off me! Take this off, take this off!" An intense scene of abandoned bride heartbreak that we've seen in a few formats, but never with this modern twist. Beyond the sad, she's relieved at the cancellation of her wedding and the evaporation of her future with this man. The altar breakup is in many ways the ultimate breakup, and here we watch the magnified choister reaction.

Such stories are the new elevator music for choister walk-up apartments. We honestly don't want to settle down before we've backpacked across Tunisia, saved the native truffula trees from deforestation, had a sexual dalliance with someone terribly ill-suited, and/or built a yurt with our bare hands. And anyone who even suggests otherwise just proves they don't understand the beautiful being that we are.

So, looking at all these examples and options before her, what's a choister girl to do when blinded by the gleam of commitment in her wonderful partner's eyes?

Fight or flight, sister.

Based on research methods varying from ethnographic interviews to debates over beer pong, we've come up with the Top Six Reasons Choisters Break Up:

I. Not the One

This is the breakup little black dress since it works for every occasion except that one with the white gown. Maybe the fireworks never really fired when you first kissed or your partner never did figure out a way to grow taller or appreciate your love for Hawaiian music (slack key guitar *does* have a special rhythm). When rumors start circulating that he's thinking of moving to be closer to you, it's time to take stock. Is this fellow really the man you want to fight with about private school tuition in ten years? He's been great as a boyfriend, but is he more than that?

2. Major, Obvious Lifestyle or Personality Differences That Should Have Come Up on the First Date if You Had Been Thinking Even a Little Bit About Marriage (i.e., Religion, Politics, Sexual Orientation)

When not dating with the dulcet tones of Ben Harper's "Forever" in your mind, choisters seem happy to ignore facts that you should probably be looking out for. Read: You're Wiccan and he's Jewish; you like men and so does he; he lights things on fire and you don't—you get the picture. When these kinds of relationships go on for long enough, "next step" questions inevitably arise, and "next step" answers inevitably follow, such as GET OUT NOW or HELL NO. One of our friends, for example, had the midtwenties tendency to date horribly inappropriate people "for kicks" only to wake up disoriented a year later on deflated air mattresses with very misguided proposals on her hands.

3. Beginning of School/Job in a Different City/Time Zone

If you're in Manhattan and your sweetie is starting grad school in D.C., y'all have to work some magic to make sure that commute doesn't wear you down. But it often does, and therein lies the breakup. Angelica S. had moved to Mexico and fallen for Juan when work obligations called her back to California. "We both knew we'd rather be together, but timing/ distance/places in life just made our relationship completely unrealistic," she says. "We made no promises to keep in touch, no plans to see each other or speak again. It was a clean break, and while it was hard and I missed him dearly, there was no resentment or anger. Just sadness at our timing." Not everyone is so lucky. Often the breakup is preceded by months of slow and steady decline revealed only through coded phrases like "I just feel at home in the developing world" and "I miss you oodles!" over late night Skype sessions.

4. Need to Explore

In an interview with Bookreporter.com, Elizabeth Gilbert, author of the bestseller *Eat, Pray, Love*, recalls her own tension between romance and travel and the ultimate decision to give up the first for the second: "I went on a trip to New Zealand for *GQ* magazine right before I turned 30 and I remember weeping on a beach while I was there, thinking, 'This is the last time in my life I will ever do anything like this.' My love for travel and exploration was so huge that losing it was an unbearable heartache. So, as hard as it was (and it was hard) for me to leave my marriage, I find it difficult to express the vastness of my relief and joy and happiness and excitement when I realized that I had the rest of my life ahead of me, free to be who I actually am."[1] Your authors, along with millions of Elizabeth Gilbert groupies out there, can identify with this feeling. But understand that it doesn't take an international flight to earn the rights to this plotline. There's plenty of exploring available wherever you are.

5. Need to Find Self

Another revamped classic: "It's not you, it's me" for the modern age. That phrase was enough before, but now we can personalize it with discussions about the specific parts of "me" we need to get to know better. Part of the problem with choisters' whole fake marriage tendency, and the ability to date lots of different guys without having to wear the Slut cap, is that Choister Cathy can suddenly realize she hasn't slept alone in about ten years. So odds are that at some point in the postcollege/premarriage dating gap, this choister will have to take a little break to learn what it's like to go to the movies solo and how to cook her own eggs.

6. Let's Put a Pin in This

For a group of people not too concerned about timelines, we sure care a lot about timing. How often have you heard that Choister X was an amazing person, but "I was working too hard," "he was going through the application process," or "she just needed to grow up a bit more?" In that case, the breakup goes a little something like, "I think you're the person I want to end up with, but I can't see myself getting married any time soon, sooo . . . " and that's their cue to leave. We all agree relationships take energy, and when there's so much going on in each choister life, it can be horribly frustrating to meet the right person and be too tired to care.

It's a nicely broad list, but there's no way for it to be exhaustive, since choisters everywhere are always coming up with new reasons to end outwardly qualified relationships. But if the stated reasons span a wide spectrum, there is a connecting message: It's not so much that the relationship is wrong, it's that something else might be more right.

DURING: A CHOISTER BREAKUP IN FIVE ACTS

So we say different words when the big moment comes, but is this just new reasoning for old behavior? Is the old dog doing the same tricks with a different marketing team? Let's see . . .

Act 1: In which the Breakupper explains what is going on in her (or his . . . but we had to pick a gender) life/head/emotional space that requires a separation. Breakupper includes an explanation of why this is actually the best thing for both parties (even if the Breakupee has not yet realized it). Breakupper promises this is step one toward both individuals fulfilling their goals of Ultimate Life Happiness.

Act 2: In which the Breakupee realizes he is being broken up with. He points out that the Breakupper's emotional space is not all that different than it was a week ago, when she decided to move in together/visit future in-laws/buy large plants that require lots of care. The Breakupee tries to reason with the Breakupper while simultaneously not invalidating the Breakupper's feelings—which are, of course, treated as legitimate since the Breakupee loves said Breakupper and is generally respectful.

Act 3: In which the Breakupper holds her ground in the face of the Breakupee's logic and remains calm (though racked with guilt) while the Breakupee moves with increasing panic from rational points to low blows, before finally shuffling away in tears.

Act 4: In which both parties realize the breakup is actually happening and so begin to mutually mourn the relationship as it was in its happier days. Both parties act as if this disastrous breakup were a thing outside their control that the world has done TO them and that they were desperately fighting off with the physical and emotional strength of true samurai. The Breakupper feels she had no choice and therefore must decide that both individuals will be truly better off in the long run, resulting in a smugness that grates on the already fragile Breakupee. The Breakupee alternately wants the Breakupper completely out of his life or wants to see the Breakupper occasionally for extensive rehashing of already rehashed conversations that will only lead to more rehashing and maybe postbreakup sex. This is a particularly complicated little dance, full of peaks and valleys that dizzy even the most seasoned emotional roller-coaster riders.

Act 5 (optional ending): In which the Breakupper repents or the Breakupee begs and suddenly they are rejoined. They date again. They break up again. This continues until they reach a legitimate END. (scene)

THE BAD, THE SAD, AND THE UGLY

So what does this play look like in real life? What makes each choister breakup seem so special? As Elizabeth B., twenty-seven, says, "There are many kinds of breakups, and it usually depends on what side of it you're on. The breakups when one of you genuinely cares are hard, and the breakups when the one who cares doesn't see it coming are the worst."

Whether you're breaking up with someone for one of the above-mentioned reasons or for reasons we couldn't even fathom because of the unique choister complexity of your particular situation, it doesn't matter. You still need to know how to do it, right? There are many ways to deliver the blow, and few are easy. The ones we unilaterally *don't* endorse, however, involve the use of PDAs, iPhones, and that very World Wide Web as your primary mode of message delivery.

We all heard the one about breaking up via Post-it note and were appropriately shocked at the cowardice. But as authors, we've (shamefully) guest-starred in a few of our own phone, email, and text breakups. All were lame. All were easy outs. It's true—we have used technology's magic for evil.

In traumatic situations, which breakups are, people have the tendency to focus on their own survival. Therefore, we become most concerned with how to minimize the breakup's blow to our own delicate psyche. Technology makes it possible to hold the entire event at arm's length, and with the invention of mass communication, we can basically act out the equivalent to Suzie-finds-out-she's-been-dumped-when-she-sees-her-boyfriend-making-out-with-the-head-cheerleader on a massive scale that maximizes humiliation, but keeps us from having to see the person's face. Why else would Facebook create alerts for when someone's relationship status changes? What easier way to break up than to click a few buttons and instantly send an email saying you're single to all your mutual friends?

And when not riddled with distance-inducing technology, our breakups are hardly anything to brag about. It's worth noting that at the peak of any face-to-face breakup fight, we shed our choister fatigues and return to the naked ugliness of shouting matches. The words screamed back and forth in the heat of the moment are perhaps the one thing that won't change from one generation to the next. You can't improve upon "I hate you" and "You're an asshole."

Breakups don't ALWAYS make you hate the person. Sometimes they can be handled with a tenderness and affection that allows you to walk away confident that you *were* loved at some point. Surprisingly, such breakups are not always better. Amalia remembers thinking of an ex, "Oh, if only I hated him." The "good" choister breakup features two mostly mature individuals in a conversation of equals; tears (and tissues) are included and mingled. Phrases like "I respect you" and "I sincerely apologize for hurting you" pepper the conversation. Phrases like "Let's go out drinking as friends" and "Those pants make your butt look hot" are notably absent. There is no tweeting whatsoever.

Deborah M., twenty-nine, received a pair of earrings from her boyfriend when he broke up with her. Breakups are not usually the experience you want a souvenir from, but it was a sweet gesture. Yes, giving a parting gift can be one way to leave your hooks in a person, so while you might say this is sending mixed signals, Deb never wears the earrings, so it's alright. It was a "thought that counts" situation, and she appreciated that, unlike some men who might text-message "its dun," this chap demonstrated the *existence* of thought.

Why is this section on good breakups so short? Because there aren't that many, and even those are just awful. Case in point, when we asked a girlfriend to describe her "best breakup," she said, "I think my best breakup was with Matt, but maybe that's because we ended up getting married." Yeah, nothing like a proposal to heal your pride.

Good breakup or bad breakup, though, the aftermath is always a bitch. No matter how many times you've plodded down this road, it always manages to feel like the first time.

AFTER: DEEP BREATHS

Since choisters are redefining relationships and breakups in ways both empowering and embarrassing, it's natural that the separation comes with a unique choister aftertaste as well.

Given that most of us will have a higher number of long-term romantic relationships than our parents did, there is a smaller chance that the one who just walked out the door was really The One. Choisters, unlike the parents who console us, *expect* to have a few journals' worth of breakup musings before finding the person we want to marry. We even date some people knowing at the beginning that it's going to end. This is just part of the choister natural order.

As Delilah R. explains, "I think heartbreak humbles you and gives you empathy. And I think getting through a tough breakup also can empower you—you rediscover yourself in the process and figure out what you really want out of life and your next relationship. You know you won't settle for less than what you deserve, or at least that is how I feel." We agree. But it doesn't mean that breakups aren't hard.

Breakups can be soul-crushing; and the iconic image of a girl crying on the floor with an empty ice cream container nearby is more honest than we'd like to admit. If you've done it before, though, you at least have memories of getting up again to comfort you. The sheer commonness of heartbreak has resulted in the creation of an industry designed to help you through the pain. We all know that breakups come with their own shelf at Barnes & Noble, and that the majority of *Sex and the City* episodes are centered on this theme. Talk show hosts like Oprah, Ellen, and Tyra are tapping these topics like never before, and the number of e-books (just $9.95 to download right now) on how to get your man back have fueled the full-time salaries of more than a few broken-hearted-girls-turned-ebusinesswomen.

In a world of enhanced choices, it only takes a span of about three emails for the allegedly heartbroken to start recognizing all the cool new things they can do now that they're single ("Peace Corps! Or I could learn French . . . "). It turns out we all have the power to suddenly become connoisseurs of how-to classes and enthusiasts of the Color Me Mine aesthetic. But what's great about choisters is that we really do all those ridiculous things . . . and then some. Instead of seeing the postbreakup time as a void in need of filling, we tend to utilize this time to start an NGO, a graduate program, or a family (yes, alone). We invest ourselves in pursuits that will last long past the arrival of another man, knowing full well that with our breakup we've regained the invaluable chance to focus wholeheartedly on our own lives.

Lara proved this theory best. She eschewed the usual I'm-sad-so-I'll-change-my-hair-color routine and ignored every good piece of "how to catch a man" advice when she shaved her head. In this case, there was no pretending she was waiting around and primping until the next relationship could start.

But no matter where we decide to go or what we decide to do postbreakup, choisters today turn to technology to get us through. Yes, technology was bad only a few pages ago—but turns out that technology, like so many things these days, bats for both teams.

THE PERKS AND PITFALLS OF THE POSTBREAKUP WORLD FOR TECHNO-CHOISTERS

Technology plays a funny role in the aftermath of a breakup. Like a good bottle of wine or a homemade sex tape, it can be your best friend and then, in the morning, your worst enemy. Remember all that earlier talk about Internet dating, a.k.a. Lazy Man's Affirmation Station? Even if you don't actually want to change out of your pink bunny slippers, there is always a Charming Charlie or Skateboarding San Diego Sam to send you a wink or two.

Technology also puts you in closer touch with your support squad of friends. Just because you can't take personal calls at work doesn't mean you can't share text messages, emails, and tweets about the hourly emotions of your broken-up self (text to friend: "Sobbing in the office bathroom"). You can receive comfort, too (friend's text to you: "Get up off the floor"). Most important, since your choister friends are likely to be spread out over at least three time zones, you'll have constant digital support even at four in the morning.

Of course, technology can also put you in closer touch with your ex—which is less than helpful. Consider Facebook, which we like to call crack for the broken-hearted. For years, Lara stayed off the thing, claiming she preferred to waste her time watching *America's Next Top Model* reruns rather than tracking her exes. "But how do you *stalk* them?" more than one person asked. Facebook is everyone's new postbreakup designer drug, and with constant updates on where your ex is and whom your ex is taking pictures with, your relationship hangover is well-documented for all to see. Everything takes on greater meaning: a new quote from Edgar

Allan Poe is a victory, while a wall post that reads, "Yay for the beach!" is a crippling defeat.

Then there's The Phone. While it's true that our access to PDAs means more texting and less talking, it's important to hear your ex's voice from time to time. Especially when you're five gin & tonics into your best bowling game ever and want to share the news. Turns out that for many choisters, drunk is a key stage of recovery in the breakup process, ill-advisedly combining obsessive musings about your ex with a lack of logical thought and a tendency to do stupid shit. With the ever-present cell phone, your drunken hours and their recovery periods are fraught with danger, making this venue for contact particularly nuclear.

Clearly, the increased interconnectivity of the technological age is a factor in how people recover once their heart has been ripped out of their chest. But, as our parents have argued, who cares about the technological trappings—aren't the raw emotions the same? No, we say, they're more complex, like us. And then our parents roll their eyes and walk away. But good talk.

THE TEN STAGES OF CHOISTER GRIEF

Engaging in the grieving process is a critical psychological step in recovery. There is a certain pride in our universal familiarity with this process, and a certain cachet to knowing the appropriate lingo and proportions of calorie:alcohol deployment. We've got it down pat. So well that one of our friends recently committed her own schedule to paper. Yes, this was because we're writing a book and made her do it, but that's neither here nor there—oh, no, actually it's here—reproduced for you sans salty breakup tears.

Drumroll . . .

1. You call your mother as you lie on the couch moaning and eating everything in sight. Musical backdrop: Tracy Chapman's "Baby Can I Hold You." *(What, honey? I can't understand what you're saying. Blow your nose!)*

2. Your friends come over and talk shit about your ex and make you write a list of all the reasons you are better off. A remodeled dartboard might be on your fridge by the time they leave. *(Atta girl! That'll show him! I'll go get some more tissues.)*

3. You have a huge going-out night with friends. Time for that new push-up bra! Extreme intoxication combined with recent breakup guarantees a messy ending for your night. *(Don't leave your bra in the gutter... stop crying.)*

4. Your friends come over at strange times of the day to tell you how skinny you look. Things are already looking up! *(Don't cry, don't cry.)*

5. You become the most active single girl in your metropolis. Monday night cosmos! Tuesday bar hopping! Wednesday sporting events! *(Is that you crying in the stall? But your team won!)*

6. You date with the desperate abandon of a moth seeking a flame. I will get over it NOW! *(You go, girl!)*

7. You drunk-dial your ex and mumble sweet nothings. He drunk-dials you back. Importantly, you make a friend listen to his message to be sure he said "I'm thinking about you" and not "I'm drinking shmu." *(Oy.)*

8. You get back together with your ex and are happier than you've ever been. *(Silence. Stunned Silence.)*

9. Your friends call you asking what the hell you are doing with your ex. *(What the hell are you doing with your ex?)*

10. You realize what a bad idea it was to get back together with your ex. *(Don't cry . . .)*

Repeat.

The idiots around you say it gets easier every time, but it doesn't. We may be dating people we don't want to end up with, but that doesn't mean we don't love them very much, so this breakup recovery may indeed be the most exhausting part of the choister lifestyle. And we don't pretend it's not. There's a culture of support around this process for a reason: It sucks. There are few other things that will consistently suck in such a *similar* way, this many times (three to five, we hear) in your lifetime. Hell, for us it was enough of an impetus to start writing a book. A few years, and lots of tears and mascara-smeared pillowcases later, we know about the big breakups and the ensuing bad breakdowns.

AND EXHALE . . .

Through our combined experience, we can assure you that each breakup *is* a promise of something new to come. By definition, choisters are curious about what's behind door number three, so the inspirational line about one door closing and another one opening has never been more relevant. If there is a choister quota of relationships we need to churn through before we get The One, then each breakup is like a little stamp on our Starbucks card. One step closer to a free grande-size looooove.

Ruby D., twenty-four, says, "I just don't understand why a breakup signals high-alert levels of distress. I am not so cold-hearted to say that breakups aren't sad, some much worse than others, but relationships are a learning experience; they end so that one can reflect upon their mistakes, decide what worked for them, and use that information to ultimately make themselves a better person. What is so heartbreaking about that?"

The breakup is a true rite of passage for choisters and generally leads to good, soul-stretching experiences that you might not have engaged in otherwise. Travel, career, family—all are good therapy for the choister's crushed spirit, and all can become the high point of a choister's life story. It's true; in that crucial, just-(been-)dumped phase, choisters tend to shine.

As Caitlin T., twenty-seven, explains, "I just felt like I had to go through this, and so I knew I would be fine. Yes, it sucked to lose Jeremy, but was I really going to end up with my freshman-year boyfriend? I felt like this was part of learning who I would need to be with, so even at my bleakest moments, I was comforted in the idea that I was moving toward the right person."

Maria T., twenty-eight, took a positive stance on her last breakup, "not because it had some sort of happily-ever-after ending but because it was a very empowering experience for me." As Lucy M., twenty-five, so wisely put it: "Breakups are part of growing up. They make you more compassionate and vulnerable, which allows you to open yourself up in a relationship. Breakups let you figure out what you want in future relationships by reflecting on what went wrong." After an especially deflating breakup, our friend Emma U. made a list of all the qualities she wanted in the next guy. "There were all the things I didn't know I wanted when I was with my boyfriend," she says, "but after we broke up that list just poured out of me. When someone has come into our lives and then suddenly leaves we inevitably change, grow, and adapt as people." And these are the words we chant over and over when we can't sleep at night because the bed feels so empty.

THE MEMBERS ONLY JACKET

You need a war wound to be in the choister club. If you haven't dealt with breakups, that does not make you romantic or lucky in love; that makes you naive. We wear our pain like Girl Scout badges of honor. And for good reason. When a friend of ours experienced her first real heartbreak, Amalia pulled out the following silver lining: "It'll be okay. This will make you a better friend." Which might have sounded tangential, but it was the truest thing she could have said. Because experiencing that kind of hurt makes you immediately more sympathetic to the pain of others, and therefore closer with your friends in their darkest hours—a priority a choister never loses sight of. When Claire was a precocious sixteen-year-old, she announced in her diary that she wanted to "feel all of life's emotions—the good and the bad—the entire range, 'cause isn't that what living is about?" Deep. Of course, she withdrew that wish as soon as her first boyfriend broke up with her, but she's back on board now that things are going smoothly.

We are on a hunt, and you don't catch the lion if you're standing in the shade of a tree all day. If you want something, you have to chase it and take the cuts and scratches as part of the race. After all, a temporary wound—which will fade into a small scar that you look at sometimes later in life and can't quite remember where you got it—is a small price to pay for bagging your prize. Because what modern-day woman doesn't identify with a nice *National Geographic* metaphor?

THE LIGHT AT THE END OF THE TUNNEL MIGHT BE AN ONCOMING TRAIN

8

I'll get married when I feel like I've met the man who I can be myself with, who has that special mix of stability, ambition, sex drive, and edginess. Or when I hit thirty-five and become a panicked mess with a ticking time bomb for a uterus.

—DELILAH R., AGE 29

To be clear, choisters haven't lost touch with reality. We studied things like physics and biology in school, and there are natural rules that no amount of scheming can overturn. Gravity, calories-to-fat transformations, and aging uteruses (uteri?) still figure into the equation. Although we justify our own behavior, that doesn't mean we're oblivious to the repercussions of our decisions. We know that *not* making choices can in itself be a choice (surprise!), and we *are* grudgingly aware that there's "cool stuff" we might miss out on while attempting to have it all. Because, in the end, wanting it "all" inevitably means wanting conflicting things.

Like any good D. J. Tanner devotee, we listened when Danny gave his heart-to-hearts: Kimmy Gibbler is a quirkily bad influence, and disappointment *is* a fact of life. Back in the real world, Danny's words came booming back to us the first day we realized that our professional and personal lives are not completely under our control. It's taking us a while to accept this because every time the cosmos try to teach us about best-laid plans, we shut our eyes, stick our fingers in our ears, and start singing Mariah Carey's "Fantasy." But there's no escaping the question: After having tried to do everything later-later-later, what if we wake up one day and realize "later" has arrived but we still *feel* eighteen?

"Like what about having babies? Do you feel ready? No? Then how's now?" You think this paragraph started abruptly? Imagine being the lucky one of us with the mother who launches into this bit when we pick up the phone. We're sure she means well, but we aren't impressed with her originality. Babies are by far the most obvious social expectation that young women run up against when we're figuring things out. And we'll get to that. Because this is the chapter about the dark side of being a choister.

As we've been showing you, there is "lots" of concrete "proof" of the benefits that result from the choices our generation makes. But cautionary tales have been written about people just like us for a really long time. Remember the tragic hero Icarus, of Greek myth celebrity? His dad gave him a pair of wax wings to escape from prison but told him not to do any high-class sun-surfing on the way home (wax wings might melt, you see). So what did Iccy do? He aimed too high, flew too close to the sun, and plunged into the sea. Moral of this story? You can't have everything, nitwit. Isn't it enough just to get out of jail? Or, translated for the modern choister, isn't it enough to just have healthy, happy kids? Do you really need the brilliant career and equal opportunity partner as well? Choisters say yes, we do need everything. And yes, we'll fight tooth and nail—against scientific fact, social convention, time, you name it—to get what we want.

NOT AS EASY AS IT LOOKS

No surprise to those of us who are living it, but being a choister is hardly pure, unbridled euphoria. Given that we glorify choice the way we do, we tend to think of our twenties as the holy grail of decades, and at times we've even been smug about it all. But ask your parents if they'd like to be in their midtwenties again—they'll say no. Editah B., twenty-seven, can still remember the first time she realized her parents pitied her rather than envied her. And any time Amalia begins discussing some of the decisions and challenges she's facing as a twenty-eight-year-old with her grandparents, they break out into their favorite song, "I'm Glad I'm Not Young Anymore." Thank goodness for copyright laws, or we'd have to print the depressing lyrics.

As it turns out, even grandparents who yearn for the agility of youth just might take their failing backs over having to sort through this mess of options. It's all tangly out there. Isn't there some famous quote about freedom having a price? We couldn't find it, but we think it's something like "Freedom has a price." See, as a youth, your direction is clear: work hard, get into a good college, and then work harder. But then, you graduate, and suddenly you're out in the real world and supposed to know what you want from the next twenty years. Shit. So much easier to pop home for some good ol' fried chicken (no, none of the authors are from the South, and one's a vegetarian, but it just sounds *so* comforting). Stacy S. R., twenty-five, tells us, "We're all following this path that started with high school, and then we were all expected to go to college, and we did. And then all of a sudden that ends, but you still feel like, 'I'm supposed to be on some path; I'm supposed to want to do these things and enjoy this.'" For so long, the "right track" was predetermined. Now where do we go? Suddenly we're tapping away at our internal compasses, saying, "Is this thing on?"

Usually, "up" is a good direction to go. Toward the top of the ladder, the top of your game, the top of the heap. But what if you reach for the stars and they end up burning your hands? Let's look at our friends, the celebrities (we have to assume a kinship—it's the only way we can justify all those hours on TMZ). If choister logic insists that dreams lead to success, which leads to happiness, then why are these categorical winners so tense? How many actresses have you heard complain about winning an Oscar? Um, a couple. And that's enough. Gwyneth Paltrow told the *Mirror,* "I keep [my Oscar] tucked away at the back of the bookshelf in my bedroom because it weirds me out. For some reason, I haven't been able to feel really good about it. I just feel sort of embarrassed and it brings up weird, traumatic feelings."[1] And when Whoopi Goldberg asked Diablo Cody on The View, "How are you?" Cody responded, "I'm so glad you asked. I've started to adjust. I had to go through a major thing last year with the Oscar situation. Honestly, I was pretty terrified and traumatized by all that."[2] "Oscar situation"? You mean the glorious winning of one? Not all choisters are *that* whiny, but the point remains: Self-satisfaction is ever-elusive.

Another problem with the top is that the only place to go afterward is down. And for many of us, the last twenty years have been the tops. We are a lucky generation. We grew up in the '80s watching the rise of Wall Street in the form of Mommy's ever-wider shoulder-padded power suits. Now, shoulder pads are out, Wall Street's down, and we're all grown up. The break-dancing couldn't last forever, and it appears a gilded childhood has made it harder for choisters to face the adult responsibilities of career, commitments, and family decisions simultaneously.

Generations past have wondered *if* they could achieve. Choisters are blessed—and cursed—with a certainty that we can. With phrases like "You can be anything, sweetie, if you set your mind to it" swirling around us since birth, we think we have ultimate control. Therefore, we're not only ready with self-congratulations the second we get promoted but also unforgiving of ourselves if we wind up in a mediocre marriage. "We have a choice of where to live, what kind of work to do, when to marry, whether to marry, when to have children, whether to have children," says Dr. Barry Schwartz, author of The Paradox of Choice. "But when there are 100 options out there, you have no one to blame but yourself if you choose badly. And I think the combination of the escalation of expectations and this self-blame ... can have devastating effects."[3]

Stacy feels the pressure of opportunity—when your future is limited not by your abilities, but perhaps by the choices you make. "I believe I can have a family and a career at the same time. That's not the issue," she says. "But what and when do I want it? It's too much."

SURPRISE! LIFE SUCKS, AND IT'S ALL YOUR FAULT!

We can't help but wonder, as we channel Carrie at her Mac: Are choisters always looking backward, filled with regret at every closed door, even as they trip on, tirelessly searching for the Best Thing?

Who better to ask than the very woman who tried to call our choister bluff in the first place. We've mentioned our dual love for/ bone to pick with Lori Gottlieb, author of *Marry Him: The Case for Settling for Mr. Good Enough* and the magazine article that had our thongs in a bunch a couple years back. Well, in thinking about the issue of having it all, we turned to the authority on the subject. When we wrote a "Dear Lori" request for her opinion on choister gals' high-as-the-sky expectations of their love lives, she got down and dirty and laid it out. As she says, "Nobody should hold out for Mr. Perfect because Mr. Perfect doesn't exist (and, by the way, you aren't perfect either). At any age, women should look for qualities that are going to be important in the long-term and let go of the qualities that won't matter at all in the context of marriage and family (if that's your desire). In terms of having too many choices, the biggest mistake women make is trying to take qualities they liked in various people they've dated and wanting to find all of those qualities in one person. Like you can choose from an à la carte menu of qualities instead of realizing that each person is a package deal with no off-menu substitutions. So you're dating a great guy, but he lacks this one quality, and you see another person with that quality, and you think you should go off and date that person. Then you date that person, but he lacks this other quality, and another guy you meet has that quality, so you go off and date him, but he's also obsessed with video games, so he's no good. And the cycle never ends. You think there's always another option out there, and because of that mentality you're always thinking you can find somebody 'better.'"[4]

Oh dear. Echoing Gottlieb's thoughts is wise-for-her-years Allison P., who says, "Does anyone really know and feel 100 percent confident in choosing their life partner? Even when someone looks like they have everything you'd want in a spouse, he/she could still surprise you and turn out to be a completely different person than you expected. Just look at the divorce rate. So it makes me feel that there's an inescapable risk in marrying someone, and if we expect to feel great about marriage we might end up making ourselves feel worse."

It's no big secret that the pursuit of perfection can sometimes take you somewhere miserable (remember the book *The Best Little Girl in the World?*). It's hard always looking and rarely finding. Unfortunately, this coin has two sad sides: Looking is hard, but finding what you want can be worse. This is the Oscar point in full—you work and work and work to get something—the perfect guy, the perfect job, the perfect life—and even if you find it, you have probably built it up so much that there's no way to be content with it.[5] So, ssh, don't tell anyone, but sometimes we worry: Is having the world at our fingertips creating a host of pesky problems that fewer choices just might have prevented?

We've told you about the study showing that consumers at a supermarket who tested six jams went on to buy more and feel happier than those offered twenty-four jams to taste. In another experiment by the same professor of psychology, Dr. Mark R. Lepper, students given fewer essay topic options produced better work.[6] Lepper concluded, "Excess choice is paralysis rather than liberation."[7] Although we keep saying that a defining characteristic of choisters is how much they bounce around, there are times the good doctor may be right, and the bouncing might stop. In the words of Ruby D., "Our world is a two-edged sword, at once both extremely liberating and extremely paralyzing. It seems as if sometimes, the more options I find I have, the less likely I am to make any choice at all. I'm not forced into going back to school, but I can't exactly determine a profession either, so here I am in no man's land." So what's her exit strategy? "I suppose the best solution is to have a thumb in as many pies as possible," she says, "taste all of them, and decide which one you like best. Just don't forget to decide."[8] Would that we could, Ruby.

The long list of things people *want* to do and *can* do gets longer with each passing decade, and choisters are quick to thank their lucky stars that they were born in a time when they could have babies at forty and conduct relationships with people halfway around the world. But while our parents and grandparents may not have had all our options to choose from—Gramps did not, for example, get to go bungee jumping off the highest bridge in the world at age twenty—maybe they would not have wanted to in the end. *Do* fewer choices make people happier? Although Aunt Carla may not have brought a checklist confirmed by eHarmony's years of research to her marriage vows, it did not (necessarily) a failed or discontented marriage make. A friend of ours who was dating a Frenchman in Thailand once said, "I wonder if we all would have been happier if we'd just never left our hometowns." Not that she didn't love her Frenchman, or her life in Thailand, but neither was simple, and some things got lost in all the complications. These lives and our research seem to suggest that a life without choices isn't automatically a lesser one.

And we're so busy agonizing over our options in order to effect the perfect life that we don't consider how the very act of agonizing might take away more than any slight misstep. While Chelsea P. tosses and turns, angsting over whether her boyfriend of three years will support the twenty permutations she sees her career possibly taking, her mother sleeps very soundly after her second divorce thousands of miles away.

So, as far as we can figure: Lots of choices + unprecedented control over those choices ≠ complete joy or right answers.

Sigh.

THE SNOWBALL EFFECT CAN KNOCK YOU DOWN

The other flaw with our option-intense lifestyle is that there is an increasing risk that we are knee-deep in the manure of a never-ending cycle. Cases in point: Once Claire realized that you could actually live your life dashing between climate-controlled airport lounges and exotic tropical locales, settling down in just *one* latitude seemed suspect. Likewise, as soon as Amalia realized that there were two dozen jobs available that she could do from bed all day, it was hard for her to imagine ever getting up at six to drive the kids to school. So we get airport-size shampoo and hit the snooze button.

And with relationships it's the same. Just as choister behavior breeds more choisters, singleton behavior breeds singletons. Many of us have experienced a certain withdrawal from not being single anymore. Along with the relief of having found someone you like enough to date, there's an anxiety about what you're leaving behind and often an awkward attempt to somehow combine the best of both worlds. In our survey, the majority of people said they had struggled to switch from their single life to a relationship, as aspects of single life were just! so! good! Relationships take work, and marriages even more so (as every good self-help book and *Everybody Loves Raymond* episode will remind us), and our lives seem to be all the work we can handle.

As we get older, we only are more and more vividly aware of exactly how much a sacrifice relationships are. Choisters' days are full, our nights are social, and our lives are mostly jam-packed with things we love (or actually need) to do. Ask any choister what she'd be willing to give up in a given day that includes friends, career obligations, and Pilates, and she'll be hard-pressed to find an answer. Ideally, a boyfriend is simply added on to the top of the pile, but it's a tall pile, and sometimes the boyfriend falls off. And sometimes that hurts the boyfriend.

As Emma U., twenty-five, tells us, "I do think boyfriends can seem like too much to add to the list. The thing about a boyfriend is that you only have one. You may have many friends, many responsibilities, many family members, but only one boyfriend. As a result you have to juggle the manys with the one. There were many weekends when I didn't know how to decide between the friends, my workout, my work, the many things I felt I needed to accomplish, and my man."

Allison P. tells us about her last couple of relationships: "We never could make it work. After living single in a city so long, I was always just doing my own thing and wanted to go out and party when I wanted. If it worked out for him to come too, or if nothing was going on, then I would hang out. Again, I wasn't into prioritizing anyone else but me."

We said earlier that choisters aren't *above* physics, and the law of inertia is a real thorn in our side. It seems that if we're in a relationship, the longer we go without making a decision to make that ultimate commitment, the less likely we are to ever make one. Choisters have a hard time recognizing sunk costs when it comes to relationships. We want to believe that even if we've spent six years with a partner, we will be able to (1) walk away for a better match and even more happiness, and (2) appreciate the time we had together and feel it was a productive step on the road to Ultimate Joy. But with people dating for longer and longer before marriage, suddenly the "time invested" is a ghost that haunts. Although choisters know the past shouldn't dictate our future happiness, it's very hard to put down a five-year relationship and call it a wash, even if you're not 100 percent sure your twenty-two-year-old self knew what she was getting into.

The other problem with getting older is that we (allegedly) get wiser, which means that we're becoming increasingly clear on who we want to be as people (that toned girl in 6:00 AM yoga) and who we don't want to be (Sarah Palin). And if we've fashioned that "ideal me" without the input of a partner, it's difficult to suddenly incorporate someone into the process. When left to our own devices, we start to build a life that revolves around our own crystallized priorities, and with each passing year it's harder and harder to fit a new person, with all their needs and desires, into that life. This theory extends to bosses, children, and pesky pets. All these invested parties want a piece of you—perhaps the very piece you don't actually want to give up.

As Amanda M. says of her short-lived marriage, "I had a definite agenda with my husband—for our life and what it was going to be—and I was like, 'You gotta make it happen or you're not coming along with me.' And then it got to the point where I was like, 'Fine, I'm going to do it by myself.'"

Amanda makes the good point that choisters can compromise only so much in a single area of their lives, as they're inevitably overcommitted with things they love—friends, work, relationships, lifestyle—to bend in any other direction too far. This is why the authors find the expression "tying the knot" an interesting choice of metaphor, because we know that any tied knot can be undone. *Coyote Ugly* came out the year we met each other, so it's clearly a barometer of . . . something. When a wedding-dress-clad character says something along the lines of "He's a good choice for my first marriage," she's using a worn-thin joke to lay out a choister reality: Marriage isn't her be-all end-all, and in choosing this groom she hasn't forsaken her other options *really*. Although getting married and regretting it sucks, so does the alternative of passing up the person entirely. We have explained that choisters don't marry when they can't be sure of the outcome, but our choister skepticism forces us to realize that even when you do get married, you never can be sure. So we end up worrying in contradictions: "What if he's not The One?" competing against "What if all these doubts mean that true soul mates like Ross and Rachel (go with it) are capable of letting each other get away?"

This sounds like "the better to have loved and lost" philosophy. Therefore, we alternate between rushing in, waiting too long, and needing to start from the top yet again. And despite how awesome being a choister is, such cyclic behavior can be seriously fugly.

THE BEST REASONS TO GET MARRIED THAT HAVE NOTHING TO DO WITH FEELINGS

Love and other crap aside, there are some logistical downfalls to delaying the ultimate commitment. And it turns out that when it comes to playing this game called Life, choistering it up and hanging legally "alone" (admit it, the government does not yet notice that you pay for all your poor friends' drinks) isn't always ideal.

Sure, you get to pick your own apartment and choose when you want to go out partying until five in the morning without worrying about someone at home. But The Systems around us were established by the rule makers of generations past, and sometimes these fine systems aren't perfectly in-line with our determination to preserve our choices for as long as possible. At twenty-five, Claire did some dangerous mental arithmetic and determined that she would be saving $2,115 on her taxes that year if she were filing jointly with her partner. Even if Claire's math was bad (it was), it's true that marriage comes with other financial, government-sanctioned incentives.[9]

And then think about the presents! Spit out "I do, I do" (bonus points if his voice breaks with emotion) and suddenly your house is awash in all the things you've been pining for from the SkyMall catalog but haven't been able to justify buying for yourself—the fancy coffeemaker, the margarita mixer, the adult-looking vase you fully intend to keep filled with fresh lilacs. When Amalia was helping her friend unwrap wedding gifts, she felt the same sensation she'd experienced at the tender age of thirteen when she helped another friend unwrap the bat mitzvah presents. *Where did I go wrong?* she wondered. And even though Amalia and her boyfriend may get married and receive the aforementioned gifts, they will have already outfitted their residence with their OWN cash. In this case, the opportunity cost of not getting married is about $5,000 in rather bland-looking Ikea furnishings.

And then there's the financial fallout from renting apartments as an unmarried couple instead of buying houses with our husbands and wives. It's safe to say that as long as you're single you will RENT. Why? We asked Ramit Sethi, *New York Times* bestselling author of *I Will Teach You to Be Rich* and he laid it out: "Single people are more likely to rent for a couple reasons: First, they don't have as much money individually as when they combine their incomes and savings." Although single people certainly DO buy houses, they usually wait longer, oftentimes because they are in fact waiting for someone to come along who will invest in their dream with them. If the whole point of staying unmarried is to keep your options open, the last thing you want to do is strap yourself to a location for the next thirty years. Importantly, though, Ramit reminds us that even married choisters should think about keeping their options open. "Buying a house makes a lot of sense for certain people. But it's not the automatic next step after getting married. Buying a house is not a natural progression! Before we go out and make the biggest purchase of our lives 'because we should,' we should think about what we want together. Do we want to be able to travel? Move to a different city?"

It's true. We have to think (not being married ourselves) that the financial differences between being married and being unmarried also comes down to a change in mind-set. When you have someone to answer to in terms of money, you just may be more responsible. If it's *both* your money, you just might spend it more wisely. You know, like NOT on $700 Manolos. But that has yet to be proven, and some signs point toward Lara spending the cash no matter what.

In addition to some of these big-ticket items, our extensive research into shit we want to own has pointed us to a few other items that you could save some money on by getting hitched:

- ⊙ subsidized academic housing
- ⊙ family cell phone plans
- ⊙ health insurance
- ⊙ lingerie

Immediate financial and material incentives are really just symptoms of the problem. It clearly goes so much deeper, and we are serious about sharing this with you. Believe us—even though the next word is *dude*.

DUDE, YOU JUST DROVE PAST THE EXIT

In delaying milestones like marriage and having children, do we leave too much to do in too short a window? The burden of a vacation, after all, is the pileup of emails you have to answer when you get back. In being choisters, do we have the equivalent of a wicked inbox waiting for us in our later years? This isn't to say that we spend our twenties taking naps and rolling around in (other people's) beds; it's just that we are so good at "gathering personal data" about ourselves (Do I want to date a doctor? Yes. Do I want to be a doctor? No.) and our partners that we forget all the work that lies *beyond* the ultimate decision of committing to Mr. Kinda Right.

Indeed, we put so much emphasis on the *choosing* that we forget to leave time for the realization of that choice. When Claire and Lara were dragging their feet toward an MBA, there were more than a few conversations among furtive-eyed classmates about the reality that getting pregnant tends to pitch women off the corporate ladder. As in, good job getting into business school, but have you thought about how that plays out postgraduation with all the other sets of plans you've made? Given Lara's furrowed brow from the corner of these conversations, she had not.

The twenties were made for professional flip-flopping. This is the decade when you're supposed to cross jobs off your list (Bartender? Too much time on your feet. Investment banker? Too much time on your knees.) and narrow your focus. But then again, the twenties were also made for romantic flings, so it appears we've postponed all serious projects till our thirties. Turns out we double booked.

Given the lackadaisical nature of our own lives over the past few years, we can now see that our early twenties would have been a wonderful time to have had children from a career standpoint. Lara, having spent the last few years with a flexible freelance and travel schedule, could easily have found the time to read *What to Expect When You're Expecting* and to care for a brood of brats. Heck, Junior could have been in grade school by now if her loins had been more fruitful. Instead, having kept her twenties to herself, she's a washed-up twenty-eight-year-old (hey!) entering a gauntlet of med school and residency that will not allow the flexibility to spawn before an age far past what those who spawned her have been hoping for.

Since it takes us longer to settle down into just one career, the odds are good that most of us are entering our prime professional moment just when we're starting to angle for a kid. In other words, we should have been either having babies or climbing a corporate ladder this decade, but instead we did everything else, and now we have to figure out how to get Junior and junior partner real quick. And since we can't control our bosses or the length of a masters program (Amalia asked), we begin exploring the joys of family planning.

TURKEY BASTER TIME!

So you forgot to learn to cook because of your big career aspirations, and now you're in your starting-to-wonder-what's-going-to-happen-if-you-have-to-family-plan-without-a-partner phase. It's true that women are having babies later and later, but often at a cost, and not without a little planning. It's an interesting world we live in where a choister may not have her first brush with Thanksgiving accoutrements until she needs some sperm-hauling. And this is the crux of every cynic's/chauvinist's/retroist's trump card. What about breeding? What about procreation? Unfortunately, that breeding shit does get harder as we get older. It's, like, scientific fact and stuff.

As we all know from watching ER, there are lots of reasons (all of them sure to be somewhat debunked as female researchers have a stauncher go at the world of reproductive literature) to have a first kid by your early thirties. Thus we are legitimately staring down the face of the cold, hard biological clock. 'Tis an unforgiving taskmaster. And this isn't one of those situations where people who don't "believe in evolution" get a free pass out of class.

There is an ominous thundercloud over our heads suggesting that (1) our eggs will all spontaneously shrivel up before we're ready to be in parent mode, or (2) we will suddenly be attacked by a spasm of maternal instinct too powerful to ignore, and we will head off to the Little White Wedding Chapel with Mr. Saturday Night. (The upside is that his genes have kept him alive this long, so you figure the baby has a shot.)

Both equally terrifying prospects, if you ask any self-respecting choister.

So what is the answer? Do we really think we're immune to evil biology? No—we are just conflicted.

Virginia H., twenty-five, says, "I have these things in my head that I didn't even know were there. Like an idea of where I will be when I'm thirty, which I didn't realize I had been thinking about from a young age. And now I'm getting closer and closer, and I realize there's no way I'm going to be where I thought I would be. And I'm embarrassed to admit that 'cause I don't think of myself as someone who's so rigid and does all this planning. And I realize that I've internalized all this stuff about where I should be by now."

Meg R., twenty-nine, tell us, "I know I wouldn't settle for anything less than what I want in the next ten years, but I can't even imagine what it will be like when I'm fifty. And what if I'm thinking to myself, *Yeah, I have a great career, but that's not everything.* And all of a sudden I'm super fucking lonely. I feel like by then I may be like, *Why didn't I settle and just have a kid with a decent guy?*"

Yes, we've heard and read all those studies that inspire fear in our twentysomething souls about how we'll never have what we really want (read: children) if we don't get our shit together (read: get married) by the age of thirty. And while our feminist viewpoint finds it incredibly wrong to put this kind of undue pressure on women, a small piece of our heart trembles to think that the fallout might be true. And we do talk about it amongst ourselves, passing lots of "Don't be silly, my older sister had a baby at forty-two"-type advice before slipping away to Google "wombs + wrinkles."

Maria T., twenty-eight, explains, "I think I used to be more focused on having a child by thirty than I am now. I read a book about how having children in one's twenties was physically the healthiest for both mom and baby, so that got me all uptight a few years ago. However, as I draw nearer to thirty I think I feel mellower about it all. The new target is age thirty-five. I also had a conversation recently with a woman who described getting pregnant for the first time at thirty-seven. She said she had waited long enough to become a mom so that when she finally had a baby not only was she ecstatic about the child but she also had a really clear sense of who she was as an individual and of who she and her husband were as a couple."

Clearly, there are lots of mixed messages. So let's zoom right in on the world that, reproductively speaking, we choisters inhabit. If we're talking about science, let's be intellectual. Let's make a grid. We'll talk about all the reasons people wait to have kids and all the reason people think that's a bad idea. But it's not as boring as you'd think—it has famous people on it.

WAIT!!!!!	We want kids NOW!
Birth control = sexual freedom	Birth control = too many hormones for too long leading to fertility/other physical problems
Lots of people are having more babies at later ages than ever before	Breed by thirty or live with the guilt of harming your babies
Advancements in: IVF, sperm bank, egg freezing	Meet him and beat him into breeding with you! If you don't have him, you can't have the kids!
Adoption, single motherhood	Technological interventions are expensive
Marcia Cross, Calista Flockhart, Jennifer Lopez	Victoria Beckham, Katie Holmes

Yes, our grid starts out fact-based and eventually disintegrates into celebrity pitting. Ah well, we can't help it. Because quite frankly this is the evidence that helps us decide, and it is the way girls today are thinking. Yes, Aunt Sally couldn't have kids at forty, but Susie down the block did, and we've basically got a similar build except she drinks like a fish, so. . . . And these are the calculations we're left with. Maybe we'll be one of the lucky ones. Haven't we been up to this point?

Realistically, choisters live in a world where our reproductive choices are not clear, in part because there are just so many of them. We see all of them playing out before us, assuring us that the old doomsday tales will not apply, and thereby complicating everything by validating anything. But that does not mean there aren't real risks and inevitable heartbreak waiting for us down the line. What if, five years from now, we find out that twenty-plus years of birth control caused our fallopian tubes to play twister with each other and we lose?

Every time Amalia goes to the doctor she asks if her eggs still look healthy, no matter how many times she's told that they can't determine that from a throat swab. And we're pretty sure that somewhere on Claire's laptop is an Excel spreadsheet with the ages and marriage/baby dates of everyone she's ever met. (Test her! She's like a circus monkey with a timeline.) The clock is ticking. But then again, so is the timer on your boss's watch as he decides who among his crew is going to get the promotion.

So, to sum up: blech.

SO WHAT'S THE POINT?

When you add it all up—the career, the marriage, the children—it seems that we're just trying to find a way to jam together different jigsaw pieces. But that is our specialty, after all. When Claire was a child, and her mother was looking for signs of intellect, she brought out the puzzles. Sadly, Claire disappointed on all accounts—banging together nonmatching pieces and then proudly proclaiming the puzzle done. And we're all still doing it. The general choister plan, as we know it, is to sleep around with the hot thighs of our twenties, find meaningful careers in our thirties, and still wake up with Mr. Right and a brood of Right-lets in our forties. But is that so wrong?

Hell no. And it's not impossible either.

To hear that it isn't (impossible) we turned to one of our idols—intrepid travel writer Gayle Forman—to ask if having it all really is possible. More shocking than the fact that Forman responded to our illiterate email was the fact that what she said made our cold, trembling hearts fill with joy and hope. We asked something along the lines of "How do you choose A when you want B and C also and then D is knocking on the door and E is really hot and F is my dream job and Bali is still THERE?!!!?"

Calmly, Forman (a.k.a. girl-done-everything-and-gone-and-had-a-family-too) responded: "Life is fluid. You don't have a singular passion that rules you constantly, and as you move through life, you continually make certain decisions and choose certain priorities. Often those choices seem very black-and-white: I am giving up A to commit to B. It seemed that way to me when I had my first child. I had recently gone around the world and written a book about it. I had a career as a journalist, but suddenly I had a baby. I couldn't be a world traveler and the kind of mother I wanted to be (at least not with a young child). So I made a choice. No more traveling, which for all intents and purposes meant no more journalism, or the kind I'd done. So I gave up a gratifying career and the escapist joys of travel. I still had to make a living. I wasn't sure how I was going to do that. One door closes, another opens, or in my case, blows right off the hinges. I wound up writing a young adult novel and found a career that was way more gratifying than my previous one had been. So, without ever meaning to, I have found a successful, gratifying career that I can manage while raising two children. But the irony is, I wouldn't have had this life had I not hit a certain fork in the road and made a turn, made a choice, picked a priority, and decided that I couldn't have it all, and that I actually didn't want to." We may be older when we have kids, and that can pose a problem, but we are also forcing the world to better understand the demands of modern women. Chin up, choister, 'cuz it's catching on.

Like talkin' 'bout any good revolution, it don't come easy. This time of life is a challenge no matter the generation, because it's when you're supposed to be piecing together the parts (job, lifestyle, and mate) that you'll live with for the rest of your life. The pressure's on. Add to that our extraordinarily high expectations and our insistence on holding out for the best, and we've got one messy breakfast burrito on our hands. But we'll risk the embarrassment of a little egg on our face for a shot at living the lives we've imagined.

CONCLUSION:
Where Is the Off Switch?

I t's time to start rolling the credits. An epic book it was, we can all agree, but this work of staggering genius will not be heartbreaking. It ends like it began—on a positive note. We aimed to celebrate the uniqueness of our generation, and that is exactly how we will fade out. Since credits always run to music, imagine us humming for you the most rockin' closing anthem in our repertoire: Green Day's "Time of Your Life."

While that's happening, let's take stock of the world we've just described. It's one in which opportunity no longer demurely knocks on your door once or twice a lifetime, but instead beats down every barrier we can construct. Choisters are in triage mode. But is it really possible to fit it all in: the whale-saving career, a weekly girls' night out, that backpack of wanderlust, and a wonderful partner we can't live without?

We say yes! At least it can't hurt to try.

And for once, we don't have much choice in the matter: That need to go for the moon is built into our wiring. Our parents used the idealism that inspired Books Not Bombs to seek out relationships *surpassing* those of their parents, and we can't help but follow suit. As our beloved Carrie Bradshaw said in one particularly relatable episode of *Sex and the City* (oh heck, it's like astrology—you see yourself in *every* episode), we are all "looking for love. Real love. Ridiculous, inconvenient, consuming, can't-live-without-each-other love." This ideal is the only thing we will settle for. For us, fictional Carrie is spouting mandates, not musings.

And we don't just *want* this. We feel like we don't have a good excuse to end up with anything less. In the game of "Who will George Clooney date next week?" there are both commoners constructing fantasies from bedroom posters and actresses who are merely a couple cast parties away from the ungettable get. Choisters predictably cast ourselves as the lucky actress, with all types of Clooney equivalents lying just out of reach. We are ruled by the notion that we *can,* and so we *must.* The awareness makes it harder—because when you're closer to mind-blowing joy than anyone has been before, not achieving it seems, well, almost criminal. From where we're standing, we've been given so many rights it's just wrong *not* to be madly in love with our life and the person we choose to share it with.

But a wealth of things to choose from hasn't made us good at choosing. After all, "choosing"—a word that immediately unfolds into imaginings of future regret—serves mostly to eliminate choices. We've worked painstakingly to construct a happy little tower of possibility from which we can look out onto our future.

But theoretically, with every choice we remove potential chances for perfect happiness, and we're worried that our tower will start looking like the end of a long night of Jenga—unstable, unenjoyable, and about five seconds away from being a mess you have to clean up.

It is hard *not* taking advantage of what is available to you. Just ask any president and/or his intern. Or one of your friends about the breakfast buffet in your college dorm, or the bar at your BFF's Vegas bachelorette party—when the options are endless, your eyes tend to be bigger than they should be. In every example, you are left wishing you'd made different choices within a few hours. These days, life is overflowing with options, and choisters can't stand to spill a drop. This is, of course, why choisters also suck at *The Price Is Right*. We're likely to be too busy mourning the ugly-but-ungotten dining room table set to fully enjoy our $14,299 Jet Ski package.

But consider it from a different angle. Maybe making a choice doesn't eliminate choices—perhaps each decision is just a qualifying round for the more advanced level of options. Just think—if you get married, you can be indecisive about where to live, what house to buy, how much to work, and how to raise your kids. Or if you don't tie that knot, you can still be indecisive about where to live, what house to buy, how much to work, and how to raise your kids. So if it's choice you want—and as a choister you do—then it's important for you to know that no matter what, it's not going anywhere. Choice is your partner for life.

The three of us have written a whole book about the difficulties of choosing a spouse in this world of options, but perhaps our children will one day tweet a tome about the difficulties partners face choosing embryos—the Paul Newman blue-eyed version or the Katie Holmes hazel? Or maybe they'll scratch the whole "partner" concept—given the state of marriage today, maybe our descendents will just enjoy polyamory with robots. *Hot* robots.

But enough predictions. In the here and now let's help you navigate the issues we have so enjoyed identifying without thought of resolution. Here's how we see it: If choices will always haunt us and there's no way to ever be sure of a decision, the only way to find the *right* choice is to stop regretting and fretting the choices you've chosen. Instead of theoretical angst, let's fight against the very terrifying reality that we could be second-guessing ourselves right out of the *best years of our life*. We can't change our decision-making process, so let's adjust what attitude we bring to the table.

For all our concerns about right and wrong choices, perhaps the truth of it is you have to just make a choice in the end—not knowing if it's right or wrong—and then make it work for you. There's nothing wrong with having kids at thirty-five. There *is* something wrong with being freaked out about it until then. If you're going to travel, don't wring your hands about marriage, and if you're going to get married, don't scroll forlornly through travel blogs.

To quote a great line from Arthur Miller's play *The Price*, "Good luck you can never know till the last minute."[1] No amount of deliberation will let you peek into the future and anticipate that this love affair will lead to that accident will lead to this promotion will lead to this heartbreak, and so on. In other words, maybe it's okay that you didn't end up with the poet because the engineer's income will let you pursue your own writing ambitions—a twist you probably didn't see coming.

In the end it seems that the choosing the world wants from us and the delaying we're pushing for all lead to the same goal: your happiness. So stop taking away the happy part and just enjoy your options. Get married, quit your job, stay a virgin, break the lease, travel, adopt baby after baby . . . try it all! Revel in these chances. Toss things into fountains to keep the good luck coming. Twirl around in the confetti of choices, and let the resulting dizziness be the worst of your problems.

Notes

I   Choister? Why Do You Keep Making That Funny Sound?

1   Sheena Iyengar and Mark R. Lepper, "When Choice Is Demotivating: Can One Desire Too Much of a Good Thing?" *Journal of Personality and Social Psychology* 79, no. 6 (December 2000): 995–1006.

2   David Scharfenberg, "Tapping into a Generation's Blind Optimism," *Boston Globe,* January 19, 2009, Op-Ed section, www.boston.com/bostonglobe/editorial_opinion/oped/articles/2009/01/19/tapping_into_a_generations_blind_optimism/.

3   Jeffrey Zaslow, "The Most-Praised Generation Goes to Work," *The Wall Street Journal,* April 20, 2007, W1.

4   Amber Petty, "Y Kids Just Know They're Fabulous," *The Advertiser,* June 5, 2008, www.news.com.au/adelaidenow/story/0,22606,23810954-5017200,00.html.

5   Katy Textor, "The 'Millenials' Are Coming: Morley Safer On the New Generation of American Workers," *60 Minutes* on CBS News, original broadcast November 11, 2007 (update May 23, 2008), www.cbsnews.com/stories/2007/11/08/60minutes/main3475200.shtml.

6   Marian Salzman, "Meet Marian," Marian Salzman, http://
    mariansalzman.wordpress.com/meet-marian (accessed
    August 30, 2009).

7   Tammy Erickson, "Is Gen Y Really All That Narcissistic?" Harvard
    Business Publishing, February 25, 2008, http://blogs.harvard
    business.org/erickson/2008/02/is_gen_y_really_all_that
    _narci.html.

8   Hannah Seligson, "Do Narcissists Have Better Sex?" The Daily
    Beast, June 7, 2009, www.thedailybeast.com/blogs-and-
    stories/2009-06-07/do-narcissists-have-better-sex/.

9   Ibid.

10 Jen Schefft, Better Single Than Sorry: A No-Regrets Guide to Loving
    Yourself and Never Settling (New York: Avon A, 2008), inside flap.

11 Cathy Stocker and Abby Wilner, "QLC FAQs" Quarterlife Crisis, www.
    quarterlifecrisis.com.

12 Karen S. Peterson, "Dating Game Has Changed." USA Today,
    February 11, 2003, Health and Behavior section, www.usatoday.
    com/news/health/2003-02-10-dating_x.htm.

13 Greenberg Quinlan Rosner Research, "Coming of Age in America,
    Part II," GreenbergResearch.com, September 2005, www.gqrr.com/
    articles/1010/2618_COA20905.pdf.

14 Ibid.

15 Brett Harvey, The Fifties: A Women's Oral History (iUniverse, 2002),
    70.16. Sarah Kershaw, "The Fading Attraction of Teenage Marriage,"
    The New York Times, September 3, 2008, G1.

17 Chicagoland Marriage Resource Center, "Marriage Statistics,"
    Chicagoland Research Center, www.chicagolandmarriage.org/
    marriage_statistics.htm (accessed September 16, 2009).

18 Anna Greenberg, "OMG! How Generation Y Is Redefining Faith in the iPod Era," Greenberg Quinlan Rosner Research, April 1, 2005, www.greenbergresearch.com/index.php?ID=1218.

2 Mommy, Where Do Choisters Come From?

1 Rachel P. Maines, *The Technology of Orgasm: "Hysteria," the Vibrator, and Women's Sexual Satisfaction* (Baltimore: Johns Hopkins University Press, 1999), 180.

2 David Brooks, *Bobos in Paradise: The New Upper Class and How They Got There* (New York: Simon and Schuster, 2001).

3 U.S. Bureau of the Census, "Estimated Median Age at First Marriage, by Sex: 1890 to Present," U.S. Bureau of the Census, September 15, 2004, www.census.gov/population/socdemo/hh-fam/tabMS-2.pdf.

4 David Brooks, *Bobos in Paradise.*

5 Barack Obama, "What I Want for You—and Every Child in America," *Parade Magazine*, January 18, 2009, www.parade.com/news/2009/01/barack-obama-letter-to-my-daughters.html.

6 Tralee Pearce, "Hip Replacement Parents," *The Globe and Mail*, April 6, 2009, www.theglobeandmail.com/archives/hip-replacement-parents/article831587/.

7 "Fred Rogers Timeline," The Pittsburgh News on ABC (accessed August 31, 2009), www.thepittsburghchannel.com/news/2007681/detail.html.

8 Jean M. Twenge, *Generation Me: Why Today's Young Americans Are More Confident, Assertive, Entitled—and More Miserable Than Ever Before* (New York: Free Press, 2007).

9 Neil Howe and William Strauss, *Millennials Rising: The Next Great Generation* (New York: Vintage, 2000).

10   David Brooks, *Bobos in Paradise.*

11   U.S. Department of Education, National Center for Education Statistics, "Fast Facts," National Center for Education Statistics, http://nces.ed.gov/fastfacts/display.asp?id=98 (accessed August 29, 2009).

12   CollegeBoard, "2008-2009 College Prices," CollegeBoard.com, www.collegeboard.com/student/pay/add-it-up/4494.html (accessed September 17, 2009).

13   Karen S. Peterson, "Extracurricular Burnout: More Families Are Joining a Movement to Stop Kids' 'Overscheduling Madness,'" *USA Today,* November 19, 2002, 7D.

14   Greenberg Quinlan Rosner Research, "Coming of Age in America, Part II," GreenbergResearch.com, September 2005, www.gqrr.com/articles/1010/2618_COA20905.pdf.

15   Americans for Divorce Reform, "Divorce Rates," Americans for Divorce Reform, www.divorcereform.org/rates.html (accessed August 28, 2009).

16   Sally C. Clarke, "Advance Report of Final Divorce Statistics, 1989 and 1990," Monthly Vital Statistics Report for National Center for Health Statistics 43, no. 9 (March 22, 1995), supplement.

17   Greenberg Quinlan Rosner Research, "Coming of Age in America, Part II."

♪ The World Is Yours, Choister

1   Institute of International Education, "U.S. Students Abroad Top 200,000, Increase by 8 Percent," IIE Network, http://opendoors. iienetwork.org/?p=89252 (accessed July 15, 2009).

2   PhoCusWright, "Move Over Boomers, Y Has Come of Age,"
     PhoCusWright, June 2009, http://hosted.verticalresponse.com/374
     266/14da84dd2d/1463505508/ef21bcff77/.

3   Travel Industry Association, "Domestic Travel Fast Facts—Travel
     Trends from "A to Z," www.tia.org/pressmedia/domestic_a_to_z.
     html#f (accessed July 2009).

4   Penelope Trunk, "What Gen Y Really Wants," *Time*, July 5, 2007,
     www.time.com/time/magazine/article/0,9171,1640395,00.html.

5   CouchSurfing.org, "Statistics," CouchSurfing.org, www.couch
     surfing.org/statistics.html (accessed September 9, 2009).

6   St. Augustine, *City of God*, 413–426 (check here at www.
     quoteworld.org/quotes/719).

7   Alexis Burling, "Interview: Elizabeth Gilbert," Bookreporter.com,
     March 24, 2006, www.bookreporter.com/authors/au-gilbert-
     elizabeth.asp#view060324.

8   "Labor Force," *Occupational Outlook Quarterly*, Winter 1999–2000:
     37, www.bls.gov/opub/ooq/1999/winter/art06.pdf.

9   Jeanne Halladay Coughlin and Andrew R. Thomas, *The Rise
     of Women Entrepreneurs: People, Processes and Global Trends*
     (Westport: Quorum Books, 2002), 6.

10   Kristin R., "The Times They Are A-Changin'," TheChoiceEffect.com
     (posted August 7, 2009), www.thechoiceeffect.com/the-times-
     they-are-a-changin.

11   New World Encyclopedia, "Kibbutz," www.newworldencyclopedia.
     org/entry/Kibbutz (accessed August 24, 2009).

12   Michael S. Malone, "The Next American Frontier," *The Wall
     Street Journal*, May 19, 2008, http://online.wsj.com/article/
     SB121115437321202233.html.

13 Tara Duggan, "Growing Crop of Vendors Hitting the Streets," *San Francisco Chronicle*, May 26, 2009, www.sfgate.com/cgi-bin/article.cgi?f=/c/a/2009/05/26/MN6317MLGI.DTL&type=printable.

14 Sarah Pierce, "Gen Y Myths Debunked," *Entrepreneur*, June 1, 2007, www.entrepreneur.com/humanresources/managingemployees/article179200.html.

15 American Dietetic Association, "Memo to Working Americans: 'Desktop Dining' Trend Demands New Office Eating Etiquette," HomeFoodSafety.org, www.homefoodsafety.org/pages/media/PRpdfs/Desktop%20Dining%20Trend%20Demands%20New%20Office%20Eating%20Etiquette.pdf (accessed August 26 2009).

16 David Smith, "Women's Lib Owes It All to the Pill," *The Sunday Times*, July 17, 2005, www.timesonline.co.uk/tol/news/uk/article544931.ece.

17 Centers for Disease Control and Prevention, "Key Statistics from the National Survey of Family Growth," Centers for Disease Control and Prevention, www.cdc.gov/nchs/nsfg/abc_list_c.htm#currentuse (accessed August 15, 2009).

18 Margaret Sanger, *Women and the New Race* (New York: Brentano's, 1920).

19 Ruby K. Darling, "The Breakup Episode IV: Facebook Strikes Back," TheChoiceEffect.com (posted July 10, 2009), www.thechoiceeffect.com/the-breakup-episode-iv-'facebook'-strikes-back/.

4   The Choisters Cometh

1 Lindsay Soll, "The History of Marriage," Suite101.com, May 12, 2009, http://iml.jou.ufl.edu/projects/Spring03/Soll/history.htm.

2 Manisha Thakor, email to authors, August 30, 2009.

3   Ron Alsop, "How to Raise Female M.B.A. Enrollment," *The Wall Street Journal*, July 17, 2007, B6.

4   U.S. Department of Education, National Center for Education Statistics, "Fast Facts." National Center for Education Statistics, http://nces.ed.gov/fastfacts/display.asp?id=98.

5   Stephanie Armour, "Generation Y: They've Arrived at Work with a New Attitude," *USA Today*, November 5, 2005, www.usatoday.com/money/workplace/2005-11-06-gen-y_x.htm.

6   Sam Roberts, "51% of Women Are Now Living Without Spouse," *The New York Times*, January 16, 2007, www.nytimes.com/2007/01/16/us/16census.html.

7   Sasha Cagen, "About," Quirkyalone, http://quirkyalone.net/index.php/about-2/quirkyalone (accessed September 17, 2009).

8   Bella DePaulo and Kay Trimberger, "Single Americans Are Hardly Flying Solo," *San Francisco Chronicle*, January 14, 2007, E-2, www.sfgate.com/cgi-bin/article.cgi?file=/chronicle/archive/2007/01/14/INGJINGKTE1.DTL.

9   Erin K., "Girlfriends and Why We Need Them," TheChoiceEffect.com (posted July 31, 2009), www.thechoiceeffect.com/2009/07/girlfriends-and-why-we-need-them/.

10 Ethan Watters, *Urban Tribes: A Generation Redefines Friendship, Family, and Commitment* (New York: Bloomsbury USA, 2003).

11 "Friends 'Help People Live Longer,'" BBC News, June 15, 2005, http://news.bbc.co.uk/1/hi/health/4094632.stm.

12 Joel Walkowski, "Modern Love: Let's Not Get to Know Each Other Better," *The New York Times*, June 8, 2008, Fashion & Style section, www.nytimes.com/2008/06/08/fashion/08love.html.

13   Jessica Dorrance, "The Marketplace of Eros," Expatica, March 19, 2009, www.expatica.com/de/family/Partners/The-marketplace-of-eros_13811.html.

14   Rufus Griscom, "Why Are Online Personals So Hot?" *Wired* 10, no. 11, November 2002, www.wired.com/wired/archive/10.11/view.html?pg=2.

15   Norval Glenn and Elizabeth Marquardt, "Hooking Up, Hanging Out and Hoping for Mr. Right: College Women on Mating and Dating Today: An Institute for American Values Report to the Independent Women's Forum," Institute for American Values, www.american-values.org/html/r-hooking_up.html (accessed July 2009).

16   Charles M. Blow, "The Demise of Dating," *The New York Times*, December 13, 2008, Opinion section.

17   Ibid.

18   Rachel Kramer Bussel, email to authors, August 29, 2009.

19   Bella DePaulo, email to authors, September 2, 2009.

5   Dating and Mating

1   Tavia Simmons and Martin O'Connell, "Married-Couple and Unmarried-Partner Households: 2000," U.S. Census Bureau, February 2003, www.census.gov/prod/2003pubs/censr-5.pdf.

2   Greenberg Quinlan Rosner Research, "Coming of Age in America, Part II," GreenbergResearch.com, September 2005, www.gqrr.com/articles/1010/2618_COA20905.pdf.

3   A.C. Nielsen Global, "Global Consumer Confidence Survey," Nielsen Reports, New York, June 2006: 9.

4 Paul C. Glick and Graham B. Spanier, "Married and Unmarried Cohabitation in the United States," *Journal of Marriage and the Family* 42 (1980): 19–30.

5 Tavia Simmons and Martin O'Connell, "Married-Couple and Unmarried-Partner Households: 2000," U.S. Census Bureau, February 2003, www.census.gov/prod/2003pubs/censr-5.pdf.

6 Zheng Wu, *Cohabitation: An Alternative Form of Family Living* (Studies in Canadian Population) (Don Mills, Ontario: Oxford University Press, 2000).

7 Ruby K. Darling, "The Adventures of Playing in the Major Leagues," TheChoiceEffect.com (posted June 27, 2009), www.thechoiceeffect.com/the-adventures-of-playing-in-the-major-leagues/.

8 Krista Mattern and Jeff N. Wyatt, "Student Choice of College: How Far Do Students Go for an Education?" *Journal of College Admission*, Spring 2009, http://findarticles.com/p/articles/mi_qa3955/is_200904/ai_n31666009/pg_5/?tag=content;col1.

6 Little White Choister Chapel

1 Lori Gottlieb, "Marry Him!" *The Atlantic*, March 2008.

2 Ruby K. Darling, "When You Were Young," TheChoiceEffect.com (posted August 21, 2009), www.thechoiceeffect.com/when-you-were-young.

3 Lori Gottlieb, "Marry Him!"

4 Marie J., "Note to Self: Get It Together," TheChoiceEffect.com (posted July 24, 2009), www.thechoiceeffect.com/note-to-self-get-it-together/.

5 Ruby K. Darling, "Marriage at the Zoo," TheChoiceEffect.com (posted August 29, 2009), www.thechoiceeffect.com/marriage-at-the-zoo/.

6   Meredith, "It's a Start," TheChoiceEffect.com (posted August 4, 2009), www.thechoiceeffect.com/its-a-start/.

7   Mike Bergman, "Americans Marrying Older, Living Alone More, See Households Shrinking, Census Bureau Reports," U.S. Census Bureau News, May 25, 2006, www.census.gov/Press-Release/ www/releases/archives/families_households/006840.html.

8   Brides.com, "Brides.com 2009 American Wedding Survey Reveals: Popping the Question Has Popped in Price," Brides.com, February 23, 2009, http://press.brides.com/Bridescom/PressReleases/ Article2073.htm.

9   Olivia Barker, "Engaged to Marry, Eventually," *USA Today*, December 31, 2003, www.usatoday.com/life/lifestyle/2003-12-31-longer-engagements_x.htm.

7 we r ovr: When Bad Things Happen to Good Choisters

1   Alexis Burling, "Interview: Elizabeth Gilbert," Bookreporter.com, March 24, 2006, www.bookreporter.com/authors/au-gilbert-elizabeth.asp#view060324.

8 The Light at the End of the Tunnel Might Be an Oncoming Train

1   Cinema.com, "Gwyneth Embarrassed by Oscar," Cinema.com, January 19, 2005, www.cinema.com/news/item/7314/gwyneth-embarrassed-by-oscar.phtml.

2   Diablo Cody, *The View*, American Broadcasting Company, January 16, 2009.

3   Erica Goode, "In Weird Math of Choices, 6 Choices Can Beat 600," *The New York Times*, January 9, 2001, F7.

4   Lori Gottlieb, email to authors, August 16, 2009.

5   Georgios D. Sideridis, "Goal Orientation, Academic Achievement,
    and Depression: Evidence in Favor of a Revised Goal Theory
    Framework," *Journal of Educational Psychology* 97, no. 3 (August
    2005): 366–375.

6   Sheena Iyengar and Mark R. Lepper, "When Choice Is Demotivating:
    Can One Desire Too Much of a Good Thing?" *Journal of Personality
    and Social Psychology* 79, no. 6 (December 2000): 995–1006.

7   Liz Hollis, "Spoilt for choice," Timesonline.co.uk, July 4, 2007, http://
    women.timesonline.co.uk/tol/life_and_style/women/the_way_
    we_live/article2020778.ece.

8   Ruby K. Darling, "The Facewash Analogy," TheChoiceEffect.com,
    (posted August 14, 2009), www.thechoiceeffect.com/the-face-
    wash-analogy/.

9   Liz Pulliam Weston, "The Myth of the Marriage Penalty," MSN
    Money, http://moneycentral.msn.com/content/taxes/p48908.asp.

CONCLUSION: Where Is The Off Switch?

1   Arthur Miller, *The Price*.

Acknowledgments

The thanking of people isn't the easiest thing in the world. You're either Hilary Swank and you forget to thank your husband, or you're Julia Roberts and you just laugh maniacally all the way through. But this is our first time up here, so we'll start at the top and stick to the index cards.

As we—Amalia, Lara, and Claire—celebrate a decade of friendship, we firstly must thank the freshman dorm gods that assigned us to live next to each other in Stanford's manwich. Were it not for that motley crew of sixty pretty women and twenty postpubescent men playing with fire hoses, crawling through storm drains, and watching *Temptation Island* at all hours of the night, we surely never would have found each other. We have to give a special shout-out to our magnificent Otero girls (Christina, Lana, Susan, Mari, and Stephanie). And they said it wouldn't last!

And so begins the roll call of important people:

For more than thirty years, Seal Press has published groundbreaking books. By women. For women. Visit our website at www.sealpress.com. Check out the Seal Press blog at www.sealpress.com/blog.

Click: Young Women on the Moments That Made Them Feminists, edited by Courtney E. Martin and J. Courtney Sullivan. $16.95, 978-1-58005-285-6. Notable writers and celebrities entertain and illuminate with true stories recalling the distinct moments when they knew they were feminists.

Just Don't Call Me Ma'am: How I Ditched the South for the Big City, Forgot My Manners, and Managed to Survive My Twenties with (Most of) My Dignity Still Intact, by Anna Mitchael. $15.95, 978-1-58005-316-7. In this disarmingly funny tale about the choices that add up to be her twentysomething life, Anna Mitchael offers young women comic relief—with the reality check that there's no possible way to hit all of their desired benchmarks on the way to thirty.

Single State of the Union: Single Women Speak Out on Life, Love, and the Pursuit of Happiness, edited by Diane Mapes. $14.95, 978-1-58005-202-3. Written by an impressive roster of single (and some formerly single) women, this collection portrays single women as individuals whose lives extend well beyond Match.com and Manolo Blahniks.

Chick Flick Road Kill: A Behind the Scenes Odyssey into Movie-Made America, by Alicia Rebensdorf. $15.95, 978-1-58005-194-1. A twentysomething's love-hate relationship with picture-perfect Hollywood sends her on a road trip in search of a more real America.

30-Second Seduction: How Advertisers Lure Women Through Flattery, Flirtation, and Manipulation, by Andrea Gardner. $14.95, 978-1-58005-212-2. Marketplace reporter Andrea Gardner focuses on the many ways advertising targets women, and how those ads affect decisions, purchases, and everyday life.

Full Frontal Feminism: A Young Woman's Guide to Why Feminism Matters, by Jessica Valenti. $15.95, 978-1-58005-201-6. A sassy and in-your-face look at contemporary feminism for women of all ages